LINCOLNSHIRE
CHURCHES
REVISITED

LINCOLNSHIRE CHURCHES REVISITED

HENRY THOROLD

Photographs by

PETER BURTON & JOHN PIPER

Foreword by

HRH THE PRINCE
OF WALES

MICHAEL RUSSELL

Text © Henry Thorold 1989, 1993
Photographs © Peter Burton, John Piper/Tate Archive

First published in Great Britain 1989
by Michael Russell (Publishing) Ltd
The Chantry, Wilton, Salisbury, Wiltshire
(now Wilby Hall, Wilby, Norwich)
This edition, with minor revisions, 1993
Printed and bound in Great Britain
by Biddles Ltd, Guildford and King's Lynn

Map drawn by Denys R. Baker

ISBN 0 85955 157 1

Contents

I suspect I have been asked to contribute a foreword to this splendid book because I have a fascination for the ancient churches of our countryside, and Lincolnshire has some of the most fascinating of all. I first discovered this when I was learning to fly at RAF Cranwell in 1971 and I used to explore the local area. One of the churches that I had hoped to visit then was in Pickworth, but I found it locked and only managed a visit in 1988 on the same day that I visited Boston Stump.

Lincolnshire, I know, is blessed (some people see it as an intolerable burden . . .) with over 600 remarkable churches. Despite the fact that in these days they may be redundant owing to declining rural populations and dwindling congregations, they are nevertheless extremely important monuments and a vital part of our national heritage. Each one has a character and fascination of its own. Some are totally unspoilt, both inside and out, but *all* of them are the product of our ancestors' architectural and artistic skills. They were built *literally* to the glory of God and in a sureness of faith which may seem strange nowadays. The very stones they are built with seem to have a soul of their own. They provide a focal point for the village and an inspiring landmark in the sweeping Lincolnshire countryside.

I need hardly say that I believe we must do everything in our power to ensure that these great monuments and symbols of a living faith are preserved for generations yet unborn. It may not be possible for all the churches in some areas to continue to serve dwindling rural populations but, as a last resort, perhaps other appropriate uses can be found, without destroying their interiors, in order to ensure their preservation? It would be a total tragedy to lose such beautiful buildings (after all, they represent one of the finest collections of medieval buildings anywhere in the world), which took so much effort to build in a far less mechanical age, and which have been at the centre of community life ever since. Apart from anything else, we owe it to our forbears to continue to honour their faith in eternity.

I hope that everyone who reads this book will be inspired to visit as many as possible of the churches listed, and to support the work of The Lincolnshire Old Churches Trust.

Acknowledgements

My first words must be of gratitude to HRH The Prince of Wales for writing the Foreword to this book. It is no mere formal, superficial commendation of somebody else's scrawl; every lover of Lincolnshire will be warmed by his knowledge of our county, and his obvious affection for it. He writes from the heart about our churches. We deeply appreciate it.

My thanks are due also to Mr John Piper, CH. For years he, too, has been fascinated by our churches. 'If you are thinking of doing another Lincolnshire book', he said to me a few years ago, 'I should very much like to be associated with it.' I am indeed grateful for his encouragement, and his photographs. I am also indebted to Mrs Piper. 'What are we to call the book?' I said to John on one of our church crawls. After not a moment's pause Myfanwy's deep voice came from the back of the car: '*Lincolnshire Churches Revisited*, Henry.' I am grateful to her. '*Revisited*' is exactly right. It is twenty-five and more years since Jack Yates and I visited every church in Lincolnshire for the *Shell Guide*; in the meantime I have been in Derbyshire, Staffordshire, County Durham and Nottinghamshire, writing *Shell Guides* to those counties – and all over England and Wales writing *Collins Guide to Cathedrals, Abbeys and Priories:* this book is a return to first loves.

Mr Peter Burton is always a most generous friend. I can hardly begin to thank him for all his glorious photographs here, and for his company on innumerable expeditions.

I am deeply grateful to the Lady Willoughby de Eresby, who a few years ago succeeded her father as President of the Lincolnshire Old Churches Trust, for her wonderful encouragement and interest in the book: the Willoughby Memorial Trust has made a generous contribution to the cost of its production.

I am also very grateful to Dr David Crook for his company on two memorable expeditions in his own Louth countryside, and to Mr Michael Sleight, who accompanied me on another two wonderful expeditions to see churches in and around Grimsby and Binbrook. Mr and Mrs Peter Ball accompanied me on a number of tours – she surveying the county for her *Lincolnshire Notebook;* they may smile when they recall her magnificent picnic on one occasion almost irretrievably locked in the boot of the Bentley. Mrs Guy Bedford has often entertained me, and my friends, to a splendid lunch at 7 Westgate, Louth. Warmest thanks, too, to Mr Harland Walshaw for his photographs, and his help on many occasions, to Dr Charles Kightly, that new champion of Lincolnshire churches, to whom we are all much indebted, and to Prebendary Gerard Irvine. It is time, too, to pay tribute to Mr and Mrs Karl Ballaam, who have for many years now always kept the home fires burning, and worked their many miracles in house and garden here at Marston, while I have been away on expeditions.

Last, but by no means least, I must thank Mr Michael Russell, publisher of this book. It has been a very great pleasure to work with him.

Marston Hall, Grantham   HENRY THOROLD
St David's Day, 1989

Introduction

It is a bright February day: in a village not far from the Lincolnshire coast the usual Sunday morning parade is taking place – the lane leading to the church is now lined with suburban villas (or 'homes' as the estate agents will have it), and smart new cars are being washed and polished in readiness for an outing. But at the end of the lane the church stands derelict – gaunt and empty. There are still fragments of bright early nineteenth-century glass in the windows, but the rest is broken and gone, and it is possible to gaze into the interior, where medieval arcades belie the brick exterior of 1812 – a delightful, if sober, last fling of the Gothick. The church is 'redundant', and a notice informs us that it is now private property, apparently awaiting 'redevelopment'. The font has been removed into the churchyard, and converted into a bird-bath.

This is Withern – the church 'redundant'. Redundant? – when the village is teeming with life? Some blunder seems to have been committed here. And going on, round this immediate neighbourhood, what do we find? Gayton-le-Marsh: church demolished; Tothill: church demolished; Muckton: church demolished; Authorpe: church demolished; South Reston: church demolished; Burwell: church 'redundant', now in the care of the Redundant Churches Fund; Haugham: church 'redundant', now in the care of the Redundant Churches Fund. Evidently, in this part of Lincolnshire, the Christian Church is in full retreat.

Revisiting Lincolnshire churches has been in some ways a gloomy task – and not only on account of those that have been abandoned; to visit a church in the care of the Redundant Churches Fund is a cheering experience. It has been gloomy work because so many churches are now kept locked. Is this necessary? It is not. Even in these pagan days, these days of progress and vandalism, churches should be open – valuables, if necessary, stowed away. This, after all, is what they were built for. Locked churches denote a Church in retreat.

'The church of St Lawrence, Fulstow, opens wide its door and offers a welcome to all who need it: in the name of Jesus Christ our Lord.' So proclaims a notice on the door. Fulstow is an unremarkable village, just in the Marsh north of Louth, and St Lawrence is an unremarkable church. Yet it opens wide its door to all who need it . . . The Blessed

Sacrament is reserved on the altar, a lamp is burning, the church is full of flowers, loved and prayed in. It is fulfilling its function as a Christian Church. Here, one feels, the Christian Church is not in retreat.

This locking of churches against all comers is extraordinary, when one considers how much these days is made of that overworked word 'heritage'. The Lincolnshire churches are one of the great 'heritage' assets of England; yet here so many of them stand locked, even their porch cage doors padlocked, with no chance for a visitor even to read the Notices for the Week; indeed, one sometimes feels, approaching these fortress-like buildings, is any service ever held here? Are any prayers ever said? A locked church forfeits the prayers of the faithful: it also forfeits the offerings of visitors. It is a church in retreat.

Here, in our own village, the church is open every day, *Laus Deo*, from dawn (more or less) till dusk. We have had two burglaries; both took place at night when the church was locked. We have lost some valuables – but it is worth taking the risk, to keep our door open wide for all who need it. We carry on in faith.

Lincolnshire is an enormous county, stretching from the Humber to the Wash, from the River Trent to the cold North Sea. No other county can boast more magnificent churches than Lincolnshire. The churches of Lindsey, the northern division of the county, are for the most part smaller, tucked away perhaps in a remote fold of the Wolds, and built so often of that friable greenstone, so often patched with red brick. But there are many early towers here, Saxon or Norman, and those very early churches like Stow or Barton-on-Humber. There is also that stupendous spire of Louth, and, beyond Louth, that wonderful cluster of Marshland churches, like Theddlethorpe All Saints and Saltfleetby All Saints, and others farther south like Croft and Burgh.

Kesteven, or the south-western division of the county, is resplendent with wonderful churches, for here is the glorious stone: almost every village can boast a great church, or a distinguished small church: there are broach spires innumerable, pinnacled towers to match. There are too many to mention by name; suffice it to mention that earliest and undoubtedly one of the most beautiful of all the great spires of England at Grantham – Sir George Gilbert Scott regarded it as second only to Salisbury in beauty – and the town churches of Stamford, loveliest of all English towns. 'In these superb clusters in south Lincolnshire', wrote A. K. Wickham, 'the Gothic church seems to have attained a perfect harmony of all its parts: the broach spire grows naturally from its base without any difficult transition, and the tracery of the windows expands like flowers from the soil.'

Holland, the Fenland division, has the finest churches of all – a fact which has always foxed archaeologists, because in the Fens there is no building stone at all, and instead of bringing stone from Ancaster, the builders of these mammoth churches brought their stone down the rivers and dykes from Barnack in Northamptonshire. No satisfactory explanation for the existence of these gigantic churches – built, after all, for a very small community of 'yellow–bellies' – has ever been found, except that perhaps Fenlanders were, and are, a race apart, destined to lead their lives in bleak scenery, close to the bleak black soil; and in awe of Him they built these amazing churches to the glory of God. Wherever you go in the Fens, there is a tremendous church: in the Fens they sail past like ships at sea: Swineshead, Sutterton, Algarkirk, Fleet, Gedney, Long Sutton, Holbeach, Moulton, Kirton, Frampton; Boston Stump is one of the wonders of England. The list is unending.

But the purpose of this book is not merely to extol the famous and the mighty – but equally the little and the forgotten; not merely the Heckingtons and the Theddlethorpes, but also the Wispingtons and the Waddingworths, the Humbys and the Sotbys, the Hacebys and the Bracebys, indeed Toft-next-Newton and Newton-by-Toft. All, of whatever size or century, were built to the glory of God. Their spires point to Heaven: the towers speak of faith in Him.

'We believe', reads a memorandum published a few years ago by the Friends of Friendless Churches, 'that there can be no solution to the problem [of church maintenance] unless it is recognised that an ancient and beautiful church fulfils its primary function merely by existing. It is, in itself, and irrespective of the numbers using it, an act of worship. A beautiful church, whether standing alone in the countryside, or surrounded by wharves and warehouses, offices and houses, is a perpetual reminder of spiritual values. In Shakespeare's phrase, such churches are "sermons in stone", and their message is delivered not for half an hour on Sundays, but every hour of every day of every year; and not merely to those who enter, but to all who pass by. It is only in modern times that the belief has arisen that a church has to be filled regularly with worshippers to justify its existence.'

The Lincolnshire Old Churches Trust was founded in 1952 by Lord Ancaster and Bishop Harland to preserve and protect these churches: in its first thirty-five years it has made nearly 900 grants to churches and chapels – it is a non-denominational charity – totalling some £175,000. In return it seeks new friends and supporters to help in this task. Future generations will never forgive us if in this age of affluence more churches are abandoned and the retreat of the Christian Church goes on.

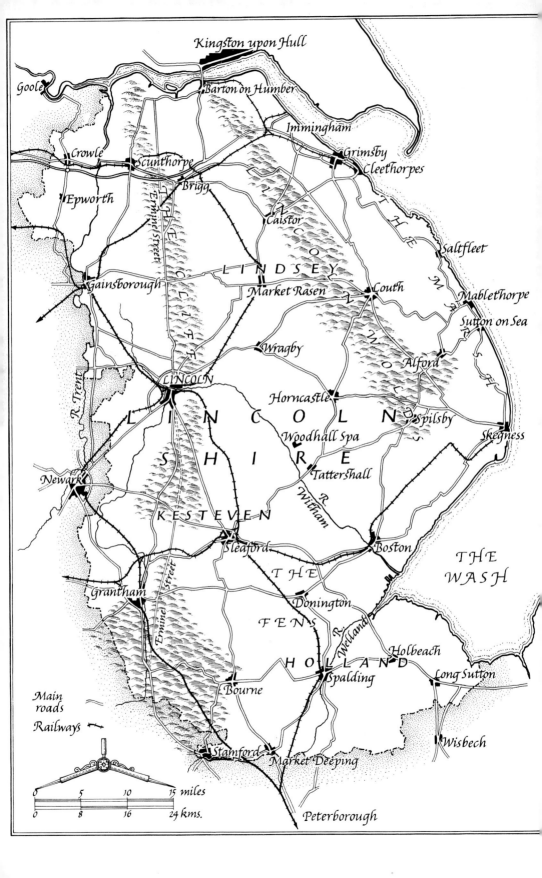

Addlethorpe (John Piper, Tate Archive)

Addlethorpe A handsome fifteenth-century Marsh church, with bold west tower, and spacious, sparkling white interior – but no chancel; a lazy eighteenth-century incumbent pulled it down to save the trouble of repairing it. A good array of medieval screens and pews: the rood screen, with its rood and figures, forms a reredos for the high altar.

Aisthorpe Brattleby, Aisthorpe and Scampton: there is but a stone's throw between them. Aisthorpe has a church rebuilt in 1868 by T. C. Hine, with a robust stone broach spire.

Alford A distant breath of sea air, a five-sailed windmill in working order, a grand Italianate railway station – now disused, like all this wonderful railway line – a miniature market place, a thatched gabled manor house (1661), and the parish church: Alford is a delightful little town. The church was over-restored by Scott (1869*ff*), and the outer north aisle added; but there are many distinguished Decorated features, a Perpendicular screen, a Jacobean pulpit, and the alabaster tomb of Sir Robert Christoper (of Well), with recumbent effigies (1668).

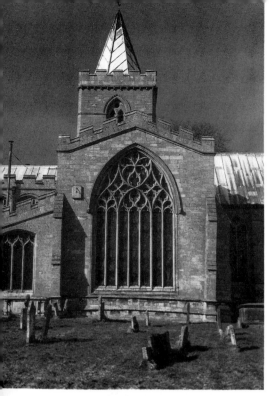

Algakirk: exterior and (right) R. C. Carpenter's furnishings in the chancel

Algarkirk This grand church, Early English, Decorated and Perpendicular, cruciform with central tower and low leaded spire, double aisled transepts, and great traceried windows, sits beside a mutilated park, surveying the Fens. It was splendidly restored by R. C. Carpenter, 1850–4, and is a complete realisation of conservative Victorian restorers' aims – with highly coloured interior, vistas everywhere, well-furnished chancel, skilfully placed organ; the chancel and south transept windows are by Hardman, the rest by Clayton and Bell. Monuments to the Beridge family, squarsons from the seventeenth to the nineteenth century, who bequeathed the Hall, and all its contents, to the living – needless to say, all was squandered, and the house pulled down: typical treatment by the Church of a magnificent bequest.

Alkborough Northernmost, northernmost Lincolnshire: walk round the churchyard (alas, denuded of its tombs and headstones) and survey the Humber – at the point where Ouse and Trent meet – and look across to the Yorkshire bank. Or walk to Julian's Bower (a little to the south west, signposted), inspect the maze cut in the turf, and gaze from this bleak hilltop across this remarkable landscape of rivers and flat lands to the west.

The church has an Anglo-Saxon tower with Early English top, Early English nave, and chancel by Oldrid Scott (1887). There is a model of the maze in iron let into the stone floor of the porch. An aura of antiquity and mystery pervades the place.

Allington Round its green – a village of brick and stone on the Nottinghamshire border; the seventeenth-century manor house has delicious Dutch gables. The small church with its bellcote is ancient, a patchwork of medieval stone and eighteenth-century brick. There is a Norman south doorway, a Transitional north arcade, and seventeenth-century gallery and pulpit; many eighteenth-and nineteenth-century monuments to Williamsons and Welbys.

Althorpe On the very bank of the Trent, a distinguished Perpendicular church built in 1483 by Sir John Neville, whose arms appear on the west side of the tower. The exterior is clerestoried, embattled and pinnacled; the interior is all of a piece, with an ornate sedilia, and a fourteenth-century brass.

Alvingham Two churches in one churchyard: St Adelwold's (Alvingham) has a thirteenth-century tower, and an early nineteenth-century brick chancel; St Mary's (North Cockerington) is chiefly twelfth or thirteenth century, and has a comfortable box-pewed interior. Placid views over the yew-clad churchyard to the old Louth Canal.

Amcotts The road from Luddington and Garthorpe hugs the Trent, and reaches Amcotts: the church with its broach spire is of 1853 in the Early English style – a hammerbeam roof inside, gaily painted and handsome.

Ancaster The broad stone street is, of course, the Ermine Street. Ancaster was a Roman station: coins, mosaic pavements, and foundations have been unearthed. But Ancaster is more famous now for its stone; the celebrated quarries are to the south of the village. The church has a plain Decorated tower and recessed Perpendicular spire, and, externally, much of the church appears Perpendicular, with its Perpendicular pinnacles and parapet. But inside there is a Norman north arcade, and the south arcade is Early English. Two fourteenth-century effigies, and some attractive eighteenth-century monuments.

Anderby At Anderby Creek the rollers of the North Sea break against the steep sand dunes, and there are caravans and chalets. The old village lies behind. The small brick church with its little tower was built in 1759, and a chancel with polygonal apse was added in 1887; inside, the coved plaster ceiling, the tactful Victorian chancel arch and apsidal sanctuary give the interior the look of an early Christian basilica.

Anwick *Cottages ornées,* and one modest brick house with a grand Ionic portico. The church is largely Early English and Decorated, with an elaborate broach spire; the statue of the Virgin, bearing some traces of original colour, was discovered walled up in the church in 1889.

Appleby Well-wooded country astride the Ermine Street: copious plantations of evergreens mark the site of the Hall, burnt in 1933, a seat of the Lords St Oswald. The imposing church is externally of 1883, though there is herringbone masonry at the base of the tower, and, inside, there are Decorated arcades, and the chancel is Perpendicular. Eighteenth-century (Flemish) altar rails; interesting Victorian glass.

Asgarby *(near Sleaford)* A little park, bordering the A17, a farmhouse with Gothick windows, and a Decorated and Perpendicular church, with a huge Perpendicular crocketed spire dwarfing the rest. An untouched interior with clear glass windows and old floors.

Asgarby *(near Spilsby)* The pretty little churchwardenised brick church (early nineteenth-century) was pulled down twenty or so years ago: to whosoever benefit was this? Charming countryside on the slopes of the Wolds.

Ashby by Partney The little church with its thin embattled tower – 'a plain edifice of brick in the Gothic style' in the words of Kelly – cuts a good figure standing alone in the meadows beyond the small village. Of singular interest is the fact that when it was rebuilt in 1841, the then lord of the manor and patron of the living, the Right Revd George Flower, Roman Catholic Bishop of Ossory, gave £200 towards its building. There is a small monument to George Gilbi (1580), and fragments of early shields adorn the sanctuary.

Ashby cum Fenby Grass walks to the church, and a row of diminutive almshouses founded by Sir William Wray in 1641 to face the west front. An Early English tower (with delightful dog-tooth in the windows), and a modest church of many dates. The best thing is the grand tomb to Sir William Wray, like a large four-poster bed, comparable with the Irby tomb at Whaplode *(q.v.)*; the families were related.

Ashby de la Launde The little church was largely rebuilt in 1854, but the west tower and spire are thirteenth/fourteenth-century; the interior is charming with restrained Victorian decoration and furnishings, and monuments to the King family, lords of the manor from the sixteenth to the nineteenth-century. The Hall bears the date 1595, but was refronted in the nineteenth-century.

Ashby Puerorum An exceedingly pretty, tiny, sequestered spot, where the path to the church leads across a meadow occupied by friendly horses, and handsome iron gates guard the entrance to the churchyard. A rugged, rustic, Perpendicular tower of greenstone, and, inside, seventeenth-century altar rails, and sixteenth-century brasses to the Littleburys of Stainsby. 'Puerorum' because its revenues once went to the support of the choirboys at Lincoln.

Ashby, West see **West Ashby**

Aslackby *(pronounced 'Ayzleby')* Very prettily set in its little valley, with a water-splash to the south – and several attractive houses: the Manor is enchanting, partly stone, partly brick with Dutch gables, a garden gate to the Green, and wonderful long borders of old roses. The church has a very grand Perpendicular square tower, and spacious clerestoried interior.

Asterby Deep lanes and high hedges – remote countryside, yet only a mile or two from the main road from Horncastle to Louth (turn off at the Dutch House). An extraordinary patchwork of a little church of many dates, a patchwork of ancient greenstone and brick; declared redundant, and now privately owned.

Aswarby *(pronounced 'Azzerby')* An attractive, tiny, estate village against the background of the Park, still the home of its ancient family. The church is spacious and handsome, largely Decorated, but with a grand Transitional south doorway, and a Perpendicular spire; the chancel was rebuilt by Blore in 1840, and very well done. Inside there are curved box pews, grained woodwork, stuffed hassocks, and all the atmosphere of benevolent squirarchal rule; old railings guard the vault of the Whichcotes, and even the pulpit bears the arms of the baronet. There are, of course, monuments and hatchments, and a memorial to George Bass, the explorer, born here in 1771.

Aswardby A hamlet in the beautiful Tennyson country, with a little church of 1747, of stone and brick, hidden in the trees behind the Hall: it is worth the search.

Aubourn A grand new church was built in 1862 (by J. H. Hakewill) – in the wrong position, a long way from the village. This has been

Aunsby: capital in south nave arcade

demolished, except for the shingled spire and apse; the chancel of the ancient church, which had survived, has been brought back into use, a little thirteenth-century building, filled with Meres and Nevile monuments and hatchments: a beautiful, precious fragment. Next door stands the Hall, a fragment (again) of one of those high Elizabethan or Jacobean houses ('prodigy houses') attributed to the Smithsons; built by Sir John Meres, it descended to the Neviles, and is now the home of the present Lord Lieutenant. It contains a wonderful seventeenth-century strapwork staircase.

Aunsby A forgotten village in remote back lanes, on the edge of the Stone Belt: only the sturdy broach spire announces the presence of Aunsby to the outside world. Neither village nor church should be missed. There is Norman work to see, but it is the distinguished Decorated tracery of the windows, the carved foliage on the capitals of the south nave arcade, and the spire itself which make it so memorable a building. The finial of the spire is inscribed 'Ave Maria'.

Authorpe Lonely Marshland hamlet. The church of greenstone was largely rebuilt in 1848, but possessed many attractive late Perpendicular features; shamelessly destroyed a year or two ago.

Aylesby A pastoral village, despite the proximity of Grimsby. The church stands alone, and with its west tower is thirteenth/fourteenth-century, somewhat restored in the nineteenth; box pews, and a four-teenth-century effigy of a lady.

Bag Enderby As its name implies, a cul-de-sac – and a leafy cul-de-sac, too, with delightful views across the Wold country. The greenstone church is all Perpendicular, built by Albini de Enderby, whose memorial slab states the fact; he died in 1407. It is a light, spacious, aisleless church, with ancient screen, sixteenth-century monument to Andrew and Dorothy Gedney (1591), a little ancient glass, and a good fifteenth-century font. The Revd George Tennyson held the living in plurality with Somersby.

Bardney The long straight road across the Fen from Potter Hanworth, the Tudor Filling Station, and then the river and extinct railway line: there is something odd and slightly eerie about the village, with its gaunt Victorian houses and cottages; the aura of the great vanished Benedictine abbey is with us still. The parish church was built in the middle of the fifteenth century, of stone and brick, and is quietly imposing in its Perpendicular way; there are fragments from the abbey, and the incised slab of Abbot Richard Horncastle (1508).

Barholm A good stone-built village, and a beautiful church, with Norman nave, Decorated chancel, and a tower rebuilt in 1648. It bears the inscription:

> Was ever such a thing
> Since the Creation?
> A newe steeple built
> In the time of vexation.

Barkston An early tower, with a crocketed Perpendicular spire – at the end of a pretty village street of stone cottages; the exterior with its south porch, pinnacles and carved parapet looks all Perpendicular – but inside there is an early thirteenth-century nave to accord with the tower, and the chancel is early fourteenth century. There is good Victorian glass by Ward and Hughes (1866) and Kempe (1885), and a rood screen (1899).

Barkwith, East see **East Barkwith**

Barkwith, West see **West Barkwith**

Barlings Away to the south is the fragment of Barlings Abbey, a Pre-monstratensian foundation of 1184; close to a substantial stone farm-house (no doubt built from stone from the abbey) is the small parish church – a curious building, with a chancel higher than the nave. The nave is in fact medieval, all tidied up in the eighteenth century. In 1876 Charles Kirk began the rebuilding, with an ambitious Early English chancel; but it was never completed.

Barnetby An important railway junction: here the lines from Grimsby, Market Rasen, Brigg and New Holland converge – and the large village is a kind of North Lincolnshire Swindon. The old village church lies away on the slopes of the Wolds, and is a precious relic, long aban-doned, but now beautifully restored, and in the care of the Redundant Churches Fund: low Norman tower; much early work in nave and chancel. The new church is by Wilfrid Bond (1926) in brick, and con-tains the very important twelfth-century lead font from the old church.

Barnoldby-le-Beck A pretty, leafy village, too near Grimsby. An in-teresting church of many dates, with Perpendicular tower and Perpen-dicular clerestory, an early font and fragments of fourteenth-century glass.

Barrowby Only the Grantham by-pass prevents the village from being completely swamped by suburbia; all the same, new housing is every-where. The old village has some good houses; the church is largely Decorated and Perpendicular, its spire a prominent landmark across the Vale of Belvoir. Monument to Dr Hurst, chaplain to Charles I; notable fourteenth-century font.

Barrow-on-Humber A decayed little town, a mile from Barrow Haven, once a thriving port: the church has a Decorated tower with Perpen-dicular top, all ashlar-faced; the rest of coarse stone, patched with brick. Inside, a late Norman north arcade – the rest of nave and chancel Early English. Wide views of the Humber estuary, and across the river to Hull.

Barton-on-Humber An engaging little town, with streets of Georgian and Victorian houses, nestling on the south bank of the river, with wonderful views across to Hull. The old ferry boats used to ply to and fro from New Holland pier (to the east); now the great graceful white elephant, the Humber Bridge, crosses the river to the west; very little traffic uses it.

There are two distinguished churches, their size witnessing to the

Saxon nave and tower, St Peter's, Barton-on-Humber

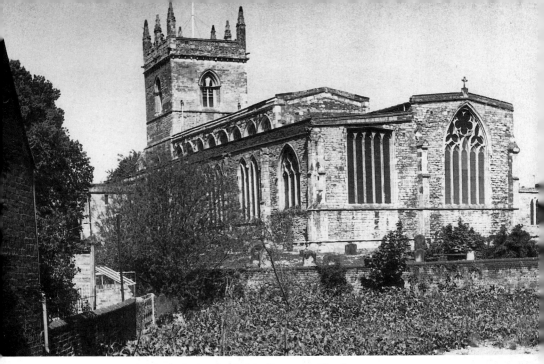

Medieval chapel-of-ease: St Mary's, Barton-on-Humber

importance of Barton as the premier port of the Humber in the Middle Ages – before the rise of Hull. St Peter's is one of the most important Saxon churches in England, with its tower with tall blank arcading, and its diminutive nave to the west – all dating from the tenth century. The original Saxon chancel was replaced by the new spacious nave and chancel (Decorated and Perpendicular). The building is now in the care of the Historic Buildings and Monuments Commission ('English Heritage'): important excavations and restoration have taken place, and are still in progress.

St Mary's, only a hundred yards or so away, was originally built as a chapel-of-ease. The grand west tower is Early English as is the imposing south porch; inside, the north arcade is Transitional, the south Early English; there is a long Early English chancel – indeed the whole building is on a splendid scale, with interesting brasses and monuments.

Bassingham A large village close to the Witham, with a multiplicity of lanes and red cottages and larger houses – and a big square Methodist chapel of 1829; an imposing building. The tower of the church is a rebuilding of 1782; the nave is Norman and grand, the chancel early fourteenth century. Victorian restoration by J. H. Hakewill (1860); his is the hefty Victorian chancel arch.

St Mary's, Barton-on-Humber

Bassingthorpe: the church and Thomas Coney's manor house

Bassingthorpe Thomas Coney's manor house looks down upon church and churchyard: it makes a delightful group. The house has stepped gables, ornamental chimneys, and an upper oriel window: it is a small building of great style and grandeur, a fragment of a large house. A beautiful garden has been laid out around it in recent years. The tower of the church with its blunt spire is Early English; inside there is much Norman and Early English work. Approaching the village from east or west, the sight of Bassingthorpe is always magical.

Baston On the edge of Deeping Fen, a pretty stone village of two parallel streets, the Early English and Perpendicular church standing between them. A plain yellow-washed interior, and a colourful Victorian east window.

Baumber: an echo of Shobdon

Baumber An intriguing church, outwardly odd with its enormous square brick tower, and bare brick walls pierced with traceried Gothick windows. Moreover, under the tower there is a Norman west door – then an Early English nave. It is in fact a spacious medieval church, enclosed in Georgian brick. A screen of three ogee Gothick arches leads to a Georgian Gothick chancel, and this screen, playfully adorned with foliage, so closely resembles similar work at Shobdon in Herefordshire that it is perhaps by the same hand; pulpit canopies are identical. William Kent has been suggested as the architect of Shobdon; Kent worked at Esher for the Pelham-Clinton Dukes of Newcastle – and Baumber was their burial place.

Beckingham A grand Perpendicular tower to greet the visitor from

Nottinghamshire as he enters Lincolnshire and crosses the River With-am; and a spacious Early English church, with two Norman (or Transitional) doorways. Dignified eighteenth- and early nineteenth-century rectory, the largest to survive in Lincolnshire, still (1988) occupied by the rector.

Beelsby The church stands above the village street, in a churchyard bereft of its gravestones – a sad sight. It was largely rebuilt by Reggie Fowler (i.e. James Fowler junior) in 1890, but displays its blocked up thirteenth-century arcades, a pretty, fanciful bellcote-cum-spirelet, and seventeenth-century pulpit.

Belchford has been unfortunate in its church: the medieval church was rebuilt in 1781, the chancel in 1859, and the nave in 1909, when the tower – considered dangerous! – was pulled down, and a new vestry (of all things) built out of the materials. A pretty spot in the Wolds.

Belleau C. E. Giles rebuilt the church in 1862 – but incorporated the Early English nave arcades and other original features. As a doorstep to the south porch a flat gravestone with beautiful lettering reads 'In memory of Oriana Michell who died August 30th 1780. Blessed are the dead . . .'

In the valley below are fragments of the Tudor mansion of the Willoughbys – mullioned windows, blocked up archways, in what are now farm buildings. And the little River Eau bubbles up amid watercress beds.

Belton *(in the Isle of Axholme)* A large village – by no means unattractive – and a handsome Perpendicular church, built of ashlar, with embattled aisles and clerestory, and a nave east window above the chancel arch; the interior is lofty and distinguished, with north-east chapel, and lower south-east chantry (or treasury?); fourteenth-century effigy of a knight, and other monuments.

Belton *(near Grantham)* 'Belton Church was built to the glory of the Brownlows, and in memory of God' (Harry Cust): a glorious collection of monuments by Stanton, Cheere, Tyler, Bacon and others crowd the little church and Wyatville's north chapel; there is a Norman nave arcade with one enormous pier adorned with lozenge motif like a miniature Durham. The great house lies through the garden gate to the south. Built by Sir John Brownlow between 1685 and 1689, it is serenely beautiful, the most celebrated house of its period in England. There are wonderful interiors with sumptuous plasterwork and carving, and

Belton (near Grantham): Sir John and Dame Alicia Brownlow, by William Stanton

Belton (near Grantham): 1st *Earl Brownlow by Marochetti.* RIGHT *Benington: springers for an Early English vault, never completed.*

some later decoration by James Wyatt (1775). Recently Lord Brownlow presented it to the National Trust, and it is regularly open to the public.

Benington A grand church. Externally it appears mostly Perpendicular, with long clerestoried nave, west tower, long chancel. But inside the nave arcades are Decorated, and – great surprise – the chancel is Early English, with the springers on either side for a vault that was never built: clearly the new Decorated nave, and lofty chancel arch, precluded a low vaulted chancel. Perpendicular nave roof, its tie beams resting on angels; notable Perpendicular font.

Benniworth In a beautiful churchyard planted with splendid trees stands a church almost entirely rebuilt with characteristic verve by James Fowler in 1875; he re-did the Norman west doorway, and most of the rest of the Early English building. Inside, an elaborate Perpendicular screen, made even more elaborate with painted figures and shields of arms at the turn of the century.

Bigby On the edge of the Wold, with the handsome eighteenth-century Old Rectory surveying the scene from the hill. A solid medieval church, chiefly Early English and Decorated; the monuments are the thing. Pride of place must go to the very grand tomb of Sir Robert Tyrwhitt and his wife (1581), with their recumbent effigies, and the figures of twenty-two children along the front; and another to another Sir Robert and his wife (1604); there is also a brass to Elizabeth Tyrwhitt, wife of William Skipwith; the small late brass to Edward Nayler, 'a faithfull and painefull minister of God's word', is also of interest. A farmhouse occupies the moated site of Kettleby House, the old seat of the Tyrwhitts.

Detail of the Norman nave at Bicker

Bicker 'From Bicker to Wrangle . . . you can be sure of Shell' – old 1930s advertisement. Trees and rows of cottages line the dyke, and lead to the imposing cruciform church, described by Sir Nikolaus Pevsner as 'truly amazing'. It boasts a truncated but impressive Norman nave, central tower, long chancel, and much else; the crossing and tower are Decorated, the chancel Early English with long lancet windows; there is an interesting Early English font, old woodwork (choir stalls, benchends), and a fragment or two of Anglo-Saxon interlace in stone in the aisles.

Billingborough A large village on the edge of the Fens – the wooded rolling country of the Stone Belt away to the West. The George and Dragon is seventeenth century, the Hall with its gables and mullioned and sash windows, seventeenth and eighteenth century. The tall Decorated spire of the church sails over all: it is 150 feet high, and with its flying buttresses is one of the most graceful in a county studded with lofty spires. The church itself is Decorated, with some excellent traceried windows, and a Perpendicular clerestory – but its atmosphere lost by Victorian restoration and stuffy modern stained glass; the chancel is of 1891.

Billingborough (John Piper, Tate Archive)

Billinghay The heavily banked dyke, called the Billinghay Skirth, protects the village from the Skegness road. The church has a dumpy tower and broach spire with flying buttresses, built in 1787 (so it is said) from the stone of Metheringham Hall, seat of the Skipwiths; the lower part of the tower is Early English. The rest of the church is Early English and Decorated, with a Perpendicular clerestory and nave roof, enlivened with some original colour. There is a little old woodwork, and a fascinating eighteenth-century Commandment board, now attached to the west wall, but once the tympanum to the chancel arch. At Walcott, in the parish, is a church of 1852, of the Commissioners, type, in white brick with lancet windows – and some medieval fragments from Catley Abbey, a Gilbertine house which stood between here and Digby.

Bilsby The church is a curious amalgam of greenstone and brick, in origin medieval but partially rebuilt in the eighteenth century. The interior is panelled and furnished in polished light oak, adorned with shields of arms of universities and colonial dioceses. A notice at the gate announces the welcome news that the church is open, and invites us to come in: a cheering sight in a countryside of locked churches.

Binbrook The church is James Fowler's *chef d'oeuvre*: it is of 1869, in impeccable Decorated style, with tall broach spire, long nave and apsidal chancel – perhaps a little towny for a village. Spectacular countryside; large, homely village, with one good-looking eighteenth-century brick Palladian house presiding over the square.

Biscathorpe One of the most beautiful valleys in Lincolnshire: in the park, watered by two streams of the River Bain, is an enchanting little church by W. A. Nicholson, a sister of Raithby and Haugham – all in white brick cemented, and even more fanciful than its sisters with its little octagonal tower and spire, its pinnacles, parapets and crockets.

Bishop Norton The elegant Classical screen, the entrance to Norton Place, is one of the best landmarks on the long straight road, the Ermine Street (A15). Behind lies the house built by Carr of York in 1776 for John Harrison, MP for Lincoln. The village lies to the north. The church is of 1737, with tower and whitened pitch-piney interior. Romanesque tympanum in west wall of the tower.

Bitchfield A stone village on the unfrequented and beautiful road from Grantham to Bourne: the church lies off the road to the west with its Early English tower and recessed Decorated spire. Inside, a Transitional Norman arcade, and an interesting octagonal fourteenth-century font.

Blankney 'Blankney stood a dead weight in the snow . . . For us it loomed large at the end of each year, and the roads of every passing month led nearer to it, an immense stone building of regular appearance, echoing in rhythm the empty syllables of its name.' So wrote Sir Osbert Sitwell, describing Edwardian Christmases at Blankney in *The Scarlet Tree*. The great house was burnt out at the end of the Second World War: only a fragment remains, with the stables. Next door is the church with its impressive tower, largely rebuilt by Carpenter and Ingelow in 1880. Within, the medieval arcades survive; there is a marble monument to Lady Florence Chaplin (1881) by Sir Edgar Boehm, and a reredos by Temple Moore; the lychgate is by Bodley.

Bloxholm A mysterious village, approached by narrow lanes, and a little church of great charm – in origin medieval, but delightfully done up in Gothick by General Manners in 1812; the porch bears his arms in Coade stone, and nave and chancel are vaulted in plaster. Alas, the Hall, the General's house, once crowned with a magnificent peacock in Coade stone – the General's crest – has been pulled down: a domestic wing and the stables alone survive.

Blyborough A long avenue of ancient trees descends from the Cliff road to the Hall, now a farmhouse, once the home of the Southcotes (an old recusant family), and the Luards. The small church stands nearby, with its odd little eighteenth-century tower, and the rest largely rebuilt by James Fowler in 1877; but inside there is an Early English arcade, and – precious relic – a medieval crucifix dug up in the rectory garden.

Blyton The church with its Perpendicular tower stands prominent above the village, a large red-brick village astride the main road from Gainsborough to Scunthorpe. Inside, a Norman tower arch, and Early English and Decorated arcades – but all over-restored and scraped. Small seventeenth-century brass to Wray children, with touching inscription.

Bolingbroke, New see **New Bolingbroke**

Bolingbroke, Old see **Old Bolingbroke**

Bonby The long road under the Wolds from Brigg to the Humber: a humble church, Norman and medieval in origin, but truncated, with an eighteenth-century brick tower.

Boothby Graffoe The little church appears to be slipping down the Cliff; no wonder the original building was 'extirpated by an hurricane' in 1666, as the Wellingore register puts it. The present church is of 1842, Gothic, by W. A. Nicholson. Beyond there are wide views across the lonely flat country to the west, and, below, stands Somerton Castle, built by Anthony Bek, Bishop of Durham, in 1281. The round southeast tower remains, with an Elizabethan wing attached – all enchanting behind its moats and enormous earthworks, for centuries now a farmhouse.

Boothby Pagnell Its Norman manor house is famous: its church deserves to be better known, for its Norman tower, and Norman nave, and

Boothby Pagnell

Pearson's furnishings at Boothby Pagnell

lofty Decorated chancel. Moreover, at the end of the last century it was gloriously restored and refurnished by Pearson at the expense of Mrs Cecil Thorold. All was done in exquisite taste: rood screen, stalls, pews, organ, a gorgeous reredos, lamps, tiles, brass gates, and excellent glass by Clayton and Bell make it an interior not to be forgotten.

Boston Boston Stump! Stump indeed: at 288 feet it is the loftiest medieval tower in England, loftier than the central tower of Lincoln, loftier than Grantham spire, and only a few feet lower than Louth. It rises from the Fens like a miraculous apparition, and is visible from the Norfolk coast, forty miles away across the Wash, and for mile after endless mile across the Fens.

Boston was granted its first charter by King John in 1204; for a long time during the Middle Ages it was the second port in England, and for a brief time the first. Its commercial importance is the explanation of the existence of this prodigious church. 'The largest and the most impressive parish church in England' (Dr J. Charles Cox): its chancel projects, elegant and enormous, into the Market Place, its tower stands sentinel on the very bank of the River Witham. The church is Decorated, the tower Perpendicular: as you walk round the outside, the scale of the whole building is overwhelming. But come inside. Here the first impression is the same – of overwhelming spaciousness. The nave is seven

Boston: the nave

bays, with lofty arcades on clustered columns, and, above, a lofty clerestory of fourteen windows either side; these, and the great traceried windows in the aisles, flood the church with light. Standing under the tower, and looking up, one sees that this is open to the second stage (137 feet), and this is vaulted – a lierne vault in stone. And from here it is possible to absorb the whole interior, up the long nave to the chancel, a chancel of five bays, lit by more enormous traceried windows, on to the high altar itself with its splendid Victorian reredos, which echoes the long line of Gilbert Scott's canopied choir stalls – the stalls themselves with their misericords of c. 1390. The nave roof (1928-31) is by Sir Charles Nicholson, the wooden vaulted chancel roof is eighteenth century, gaily and effectively painted by Nicholson. The excellent east window is by O'Connor, the pulpit is of 1612; there are monuments of all periods, pride of place going to the Fydell monuments in the north aisle – that to Richard Fydell (by Wallis of Newark) of 1780 is specially charming. The only jarring note in this incredible interior is the hideous recent nave altar with its accompanying furniture.

It is a pleasure to walk along the river bank, or through the town; the vandals have been here, but there are still good buildings to enjoy: the Assembly Rooms (1826) and the Corporation Building (1771) in the Market Place; down South Street, Shodfriars Hall (sixteenth century and Oldrid Scott), the Old Guildhall (late fifteenth century), and Fydell House (1726); and along the quayside, old warehouses.

Of the other churches, Holy Trinity is an early work of Gilbert Scott (1846), and St Thomas, Skirbeck Quarter is a charming building by Temple Moore (1912 *ff*). Downstream, Skirbeck church has a flavour of *Great Expectations*, with its Victorian gravestones and solitary lamp, close to the bank of the Witham as it flows towards the Wash. The tower is Perpendicular, the body of the church Early English and Decorated, the chancel a rebuilding by Temple Moore (1933); pulpit and font are seventeenth century.

Bottesford Now caught up in the suburbs of Scunthorpe – but a lane leads down to the old village, and the church. This is one of the finest pure Early English churches anywhere, and deserves to be better known. The nave is lofty and clerestoried, and the chancel is as lofty as the nave. There are grand narrow transepts – and everywhere long narrow lancet windows, especially and strikingly so in the chancel. In the nave clerestory is clever interplay of alternate circular and lancet lights. It is all the work of the greatest refinement.

OPPOSITE *Britannia and the Stump*

Bourne Abbey

Bourne is an ancient little town on the edge of the Fens, the reputed birthplace of Hereward the Wake, the birthplace of William Cecil, Lord Burghley. The town – brick and stone – with the tall tower of the Abbey presiding, lies below the long wooded escarpment of the Stone Belt: all roads lead into the Market Place and Bryan Browning's classical Town Hall (1821); a short distance to the south with the Bourne stream flowing past the west front, stands the Abbey. This is of considerable beauty, with twin lancets adorning the base of twin towers (the north-west tower never completed), and blank Early English arcading to adorn the whole front.

Bourne Abbey was founded in 1138 for Arroasian canons (a branch of the Augustinians): it was neither large nor wealthy – the uncompleted tower testifies to this; there were only nine canons at the time of the Dissolution, when the nave became the parish church. This is Norman and impressive with its circular piers and round arches, and must date from c. 1140; the clerestory is Perpendicular, added no doubt when the Perpendicular south-west tower with its tall pinnacles was added; what lay to the east of the nave is not known. There are traces of a Norman crossing, but the present chancel is a rebuilding of 1807, with Perpendicular windows and other old material reused. A candelabrum of 1742 adorns the nave; there are a few minor monuments, and some colourful Victorian glass.

Braceborough Only a small village – its spa is no more! The Spa House, in a field, a diminutive hotel, and a railway station, 'Braceborough Spa' – all are gone. The church has a Decorated broach spire, but much of the rest, with its pretty apse, is of 1859, by Charles Kirk.

Braceby A pretty place: stone cottages and houses (one dated 1653) stand around the church. With its double bellcote, blocked south arcade, and Early English north arcade, it is chiefly thirteenth century; the clerestory is Perpendicular. A delightful little building.

Bradley A leafy, pretty spot, for all the proximity of Grimsby, and an ancient little village church, with Decorated font and old pews.

Brandon A little medieval chapel sitting unfenced on its green, with bellcote and a Norman south doorway with tympanum. Inside, an early tub font, traces of medieval wall-paintings, a striking Decorated niche in the north aisle, and a delightful array of fifteenth-century graffiti in the window by the pulpit – the whole restored and refurnished by Charles Kirk in 1872. The Old Hall is dated 1637, and is charming with its alternating bands of grey stone and ironstone.

Branston Saxon tower with Perpendicular spire – the rest of the church burnt out in 1963, and rebuilt by G. G. Pace. Notable monuments to Sir Cecil Wray, by Carter (1736), with busts, and to Lord Vere Bertie (1770). The Wrays (see also Glentworth and Fillingham) had an interesting seventeenth-century house here, which was replaced by a house of 1884 by J. MacVicar Anderson – now flats.

Brant Broughton Without doubt one of the best of all Lincolnshire churches. It is chiefly of the late fourteenth century, the spire lofty and crocketed, the exterior and especially the porches richly decorated, the interior glowing with subdued colour. With rood screen and sumptuous chancel rebuilt by Bodley, excellent stained glass mostly designed and executed by the then rector, Canon F. H. Sutton, reredos with its celebrated picture, the whole lit by candles, it is like a medieval dream. Many attractive houses in the wide village street.

Bratoft A Marshland Perpendicular church of greenstone, with an eighteenth-century brick tower. Inside, old rood screen, and parclose screens to north and south chapels, and many delightful poppyheads – and an enormous painting of the defeat of the Spanish Armada hanging in the tower.

Brattleby The Hall is a tall early nineteenth-century dolls' house, home of several generations of the Wright family. The church was over-restored by Fowler in 1858, but the tower (apart from its Victorian lead spire) is ancient, as is the thirteenth-century nave arcade inside.

Brauncewell A tiny group of church and manor farm in fields near Cranwell, two miles or more from the village of its name – far away on the other side of the main road. It is a little early nineteenth-century church, with miniature tower – now maintained by the Lincolnshire Old Churches Trust.

OPPOSITE *Brant Broughton.* BELOW *Canon Sutton's glass at Brant Broughton, and (right) the early nineteenth-century church at Brauncewell.*

Brigg Or Glandford Brigg, as the old maps will have it – the bridge over the River Ancholme. Brigg is an odd little town, by no means unattractive, which grew up round the warehouses on the river bank at the end of the eighteenth century. There are some good houses in the main street – the Brocklesby Ox, the Nelthorpe Arms, the Dying Gladiator (with its gory figure), and the Town Hall of 1817. The church is odd, too, with its thin tall tower and spidery Gothic details, by W. A. Nicholson (1842), strangely squeezed in among shops and public houses. Inside, a lofty nave, and a tiny chancel vaulted in plaster, all pre-Oxford Movement in its inspiration.

Brigsley The church stands upon its grassy bank. The base of the tower is eleventh-century, the top Perpendicular; the nave is an extraordinary patchwork, with eighteenth-and nineteenth-century wooden traceried windows occupying the blocked up arcades; the chancel is Decorated; eighteenth-century altar rails and pulpit.

Brinkhill Tennyson country: little church of 1857, greenstone and brick, by Maughan and Fowler.

Brocklesby The demesne of the Earl of Yarborough. The park is a thousand acres in extent, and the present house dates from c. 1730, but has been enlarged over the years, gutted by fire in 1898 and rebuilt by Sir Reginald Blomfield, and more recently reduced to its original size by Claud Philimore. The family first came to Brocklesby in the reign of Queen Elizabeth, and over the centuries has steadily built up its great estate and benevolently dominated the district.

The church is a Decorated building, with west tower and small lead spire, and contains the earlier monuments to the family, notably the two elaborately coloured alabaster tombs (1587 and 1629) to the first two Sir William Pelhams. The organ (dated 1773) came from the house.

Brothertoft Deep in the Fens: Hall and church make an attractive group. The church is of 1847, by S. Lewin: it is full of dark woodwork and contemporary glass. The heavy hammerbeam roof rests on amusing corbels – one representing a bishop in full-bottomed wig wearing a mitre on top.

Broughton With Broughton, and Hough-on-the-Hill in the south of the county, Lincolnshire can claim two of the only four Saxon towers in all England with a semi-circular extruding staircase turret. This here is impressive indeed, as is the whole tower with its herringbone masonry; the top is Perpendicular and pinnacled as at Hough. There is Norman

Broughton: the Saxon tower

masonry in the nave and chancel, but what we see is mostly Decorated and Perpendicular. There are notable tombs: to Sir Henry Redford and his wife (c. 1370), with accompanying brasses, and to Sir Edmund Anderson, Lord Chief Justice (d. 1660). Dormitory country for Brigg and Scunthorpe.

Broxholme A tiny remote hamlet at the back of beyond, in the flat country between the Cliff and the Trent, its very existence almost forgotten. The small rock-faced church of 1857, by T. C. Hine, displays in its porch a printed notice from the then Bishop of Lincoln, acknowledging the receipt of the Quota in 1952. Time has stood still here.

Bucknall A little church of greenstone with modest tower, all outwardly Victorian – but, within, early fourteenth-century arcades betray its antiquity. Notable pulpit of 1646. 'No man's land', between the Witham and the Wolds.

Burgh-le-Marsh *(pronounced 'Borough')* A breath of the sea: Skegness is only five miles away. But despite the traffic Burgh is an attractive little place, dominated by the Perpendicular tower of the church, a grand Marshland church, with Perpendicular clerestoried nave, charming brick north porch of 1702 (with Dutch gable), and an interior resplendent with good woodwork. There is a rood screen (with figures of 1963), a pair of parclose screens, a pulpit of 1623, and a remarkable font cover, crowned with a bird holding a mysterious bottle. A beautifully furnished, devotional interior.

Burgh-on-Bain *('Borough-le-Marsh', but 'Brough-on-Bain')* The church sits astride the Louth road, above the valley of the infant Bain; there is a Norman tower arch, and a good Early English nave arcade. Much restoration of 1874, and much decoration too, with scrolly Victorian texts. Under the tower a monument by Scheemakers to Thomas Pindar of Girsby (1741).

Burringham Close to the Trent; S. S. Teulon's church (1857) is Teulon at his most assertive – indeed altogether a very curious building, with low west tower with steep pyramid roof, and apsidal east end, all in red and black brick. It is highly original: who else but Teulon could have given it to us? It is now in the care of the Redundant Churches Fund.

Burton-by-Lincoln The little church with its seventeenth-century tower lies on the edge of the park: it is in fact late eighteenth-century, but was Gothicised in the nineteenth. The eighteenth-century gallery is the Monson family pew, with its fireplace and upholstery. Only the south front

Burgh-le-Marsh

of the Hall (James Paine, 1768) survives, since the Monsons moved back to their original home at South Carlton (next door) after the Second World War.

Burton Coggles 'Coggle' is the Lincolnshire equivalent of 'cobble', a small round stone. The dumpy little thirteenth-century broach spire is an endearing sight from the railway, surrounded by the stone cottages of the village. The church itself is unexpectedly spacious, with Early English and Perpendicular arcades in the nave, and a Norman window in the west wall proves that this was once a Norman nave, before the building of the tower. Long chancel with handsome Victorian furnishings and colourful glass by Hardman; in the south aisle memorials to the Cholmeleys of Easton range from small sixteenth-century brasses to an early nineteenth-century marble tablet to a Cholmeley who was rector of the parish, and died after a very short incumbency in 1814. Two grand effigies in the porch.

Burton Pedwardine Vanished splendour: only the mounds and traces of the moats of the great house of the Pedwardines remain, and the grand cruciform church with central tower and spire, built in the middle of the fourteenth century, collapsed in 1802. A 'mean structure' was built in its place, and in 1870 the present church was built (by Charles Kirk), with its pretty bellcote. Only the north transept of the great church survives, but it contains the effigy of Dame Alice Pedwardine, wife of Sir Roger, builder of the church (c. 1350), and the alabaster tomb of Sir Thomas Horsman (1610).

Burton-upon-Stather Spectacular views from the hillside across the Trent – and the Ouse. The church has a distinguished Norman north arcade; the rest is mainly thirteenth century, but much restored by Browning in 1865. There are interesting monuments to the Sheffields of Normanby, especially that to Sir Charles Sheffield, 1st baronet (1775) by Fisher of York. Normanby is a large, severe Classical stone house built in 1825 by Smirke for Sir Robert, 4th baronet; the main house is now leased to the Scunthorpe Museum and Art Gallery, and is open to the public – but Brierley's east wing is still retained by the family.

Burwell The church is built into the side of the Wold, above the main-road village: a Perpendicular tower of greenstone, with an eighteenth-century brick top, a Norman chancel arch, a late seventeenth-century Alington monument, and eighteenth-century tablets to the Listers, who built the distinguished Hall in 1760 (filled with Rococo plasterwork), shamefully destroyed in 1958. The church is now in the care of the Redundant Churches Fund.

Buslingthorpe The small church of 1835 (by E. J. Willson), in white brick, attached to a low medieval tower, is of little note, but it contains one of the earliest brasses in England, to Sir Richard de Buslingthorpe, a demi-figure on a stone coffin-lid. It is not dated, but is perhaps of c. 1300. Nearby is the stone effigy (late thirteenth century) of (perhaps) Sir John de Buslingthorpe. The church is now in the care of the Redundant Churches Fund.

Butterwick *(near Boston)* East of Boston and not far from the sea: the church is a delightful amalgam of stone and brick, with an eighteenth-century brick tower, and sixteenth-century brick clerestory. Inside there are thirteenth-century arcades – but there has been much patching and rebuilding over the centuries; seventeenth-century pulpit.

Butterwick, West see **West Butterwick**

Cabourne A pretty place, for all the traffic on the main road to Grimsby, and an ancient little church restored by Blomfield in 1872. Norman tower and doorway; Norman font; Early English lancet windows.

Cadney A rewarding church in forgotten countryside south of Brigg: Early English tower and chancel, grand Norman nave arcade, ancient screen (perhaps from Newstead Priory) – all well restored by Sir Charles Nicholson in 1912. At Newstead Priory Farm there is one original vaulted room, perhaps part of the refectory of the Gilbertine priory founded here in 1171.

Caenby Much traffic at the roundabout at Caenby Corner: the minute village of Caenby is an entirely different matter – a large old farmhouse on the site of the medieval moated mansion of the Tournays, approached by a bumpy track, with a tiny church nearby, dim and Victorianised, with a bright east window, at present unused. The property passed from the Tournays to the Moncks, so to the Middletons of Belsay Castle, Northumberland. The Moncks' Arms at Caenby Corner alone keeps their memory alive.

Caistor has its charm, with its Market Place and Georgian houses, and narrow streets descending the hill. Though a Roman town, there is nothing of this to see above ground. The church is ancient, with Anglo-Saxon tower (the upper parts Early English and Decorated), and lofty Early English nave. Much Victorian glass; two fourteenth-century effigies, and monument to Sir Edward Maddison of Fonaby with kneeling figure; he died in 1583, aged 100. Butterfield restored the church in 1862; rood beam with figures by Wilfrid Bond (1920).

Cammeringham Not much of the medieval church survives, but the Norman north arcade is embedded in the north wall, and an Anglo-Saxon shaft above the present west door; there is an elegant little marble font of 1755, and a curious and attractive monument to Mrs Jane Tyrwhitt, 'a most vertuous and religious gentlewoman' who died in 1636; her face looks out on us from a garlanded marble frame. Of this ancient Lincolnshire family (see Bigby and Stainfield) only the Tyrwhitts of Cammeringham survive in the male line; Admiral of the Fleet Sir Reginald Tyrwhitt was created a baronet in 1919 for his distinguished services in the First World War. The present baronet is his grandson.

Candlesby An attractive huddle of a village on the edge of the Wolds, and a brick church of 1838 by E. D. Rainey of Spilsby, with a narrow tower and thin Gothic details. Candlesby Hall is a charming smaller Georgian house, built by the Massingberds.

Canwick Shades of the Sibthorps: John Sibthorp was the eighteenth-century botanist; Colonel Charles Sibthorp was MP for Lincoln, and arch-Tory; the Revd Richard Waldo Sibthorp, his brother, was ordained an Anglican, became a Roman and was re-ordained – and again reverted to the Church of England, only to return to the Roman Church two years later. He was buried, at his express wish, according to the rites of the Church of England. The church has a Norman nave arcade, and is full of box pews and monuments and hatchments. The Hall, the Sibthorps' house, with its austere early nineteenth-century façade, is now flats, but the view of Lincoln Cathedral from here remains deservedly famous.

Careby The church stands by itself on the edge of its tiny village, in meadows watered by the infant River Glen. Its early thirteenth-century tower with low pyramid roof gives the whole composition a French look. Fourteenth-century doorknocker on the south door; inside, there are Perpendicular arcades, a rare medieval crimson cope made into an altar frontal, and a most unusual nineteenth-century pitch-pine vaulted roof.

Carlby The beautiful stone country of the Rutland border. The church is predominantly Early English, with a slender broach spire; spacious interior with some remains of seventeenth-century woodwork, and fragments of a medieval Doom above the chancel arch.

Carlton, Great see **Great Carlton**

Carlton-le-Moorland That rare thing: an Elizabethan church. The tower is early (in origin Norman or even Saxon) and the chancel Decorated – but all the body of the church is sixteenth century, with mullioned and transomed windows like a house of the period. Seventeenth-century Disney brass, and seventeenth-century furnishings. A comfortable red-brick village in flat country watered by the River Witham.

Carlton, Little see **Little Carlton**

Carlton, North see **North Carlton**

Carlton, South see **South Carlton**

Carlton Scroop 'On Sunday in the night the 14th November 1630 the

Careby

steeple of this church fell and broke down the roofs of the nave and two isles . . .' So reads an insription inside; it was rebuilt in 1632. Interior scraped, but there is good woodwork, and very good fourteenth-century glass in the upper lights of the east window, including a knightly donor's figure.

Carrington One of Jephtha Pacey's little Fen chapels (1816) – attractive with its wide overhanging eaves, and its little octagonal cupola. The small apsidal chancel is an addition of 1872.

Castle Bytham A most attractive village close to the Rutland border, with stone cottages and steep streets looking across to the monumental earthworks of the castle which Henry III besieged in 1221, and which was burnt in the Wars of the Roses. The church is cruciform, with Early English tower and nave, and a long Decorated chancel; beautiful early twentieth-century furnishings.

Caythorpe Like Welbourn (*q.v.*) the spire has a pronounced 'entasis', but notwithstanding it is noble and graceful and wonderfully lofty, with crockets and flying buttresses. The church has an unusual plan – the nave comprised of two great Decorated aisles with an arcade down the centre (the third, north, aisle is by Sir G. G. Scott, 1860); narrow crossing, shallow transepts – the spire rising from the crossing. Two handsome early eighteenth-century Hussey monuments. The Hall is a rebuilding of the former Hussey seat, by William Parsons (1823) for Colonel Hussey Packe, a severe Classical house; there are a number of attractive earlier stone houses in the village.

Chapel St Leonards was originally known as Chapel Mumby, as the little church of 1794 was a chapel-of-ease to Mumby. It was then a solitary hamlet: now there are unending bungalows and chalets and caravans by the sea.

Cherry Willingham Dormitory village near Lincoln: bungalows and small houses galore. The church was built in 1753 by Thomas Becke, merchant of Lincoln, and is an accomplished small Classical building of stone, with a pedimented west front crowned with an octagonal cupola, and a shallow east apse. Inside, a marble tablet commemorates Thomas Becke, who died in 1757.

Claxby St Andrew A tiny Norman Revival church in brick, of all comic things, built in 1846, close to the Hall. This is externally a modest eighteenth-century house, but contains two or three small disting-uished rooms – with first-rate plasterwork and chimneypieces. It was built by James Bateman as the dower house for Well (*q.v*).

Claxby St Mary The foothills of the Wolds: great woods clothe the hillside. The church was much restored in 1871, but is in origin Early English – with a Perpendicular tower. Monument with kneeling figures to John Witherwick (1605).

Claypole A noble church – with lofty crocketed spire dominating the flat lands on the borders of Nottinghamshire. The proportions are superb: nave with traceried Decorated windows in the aisles and lofty clerestory, grand chancel with more Decorated tracery, and finally, grand Perpendicular east window – with more Perpendicular windows in north and south transepts; the spire, too, is Perpendicular, and with its lozenge frieze and crocketed pinnacles is a larger version of neighbour-ing Fenton. The interior is light and spacious: Decorated arcades with

OPPOSITE *Claypole*

carved foliage capitals, Perpendicular screen and pulpit, its reading desk supported on the brass stem of the medieval processional cross, sumptuous Decorated sedilia in the chancel, simpler Early English sedilia in the south transept.

Cleethorpes is contiguous to Grimsby, a large Victorian seaside resort with pier, promenade, municipal gardens, children's paddling pool, and all the amusements associated therewith. There is nothing whatever to detain us, except for James Fowler's parish church (1867), with its tower and ornate arcades.

'Old Clee', however, is very different. The ancient church is set in what remains of the old village – but is all surrounded with long unending roads of modern houses. It is a church of great importance, with Saxon tower and Norman nave; crossing, transepts and chancel are a little later, and on the south pier is an inscription referring to the dedication of this part of the church by St Hugh in 1192. A venerable and moving interior.

Clixby A tiny church, now in the care of the Redundant Churches Fund – the chancel of an Early English church, possessing many features of interest: Decorated windows, an ogee-headed doorway and sedilia, and old floor slabs. A very pretty, remote hillside.

Coates, Great see **Great Coates**

Coates, Little see **Little Coates**

Coates, North see **North Coates**

Cockerington, South see **South Cockerington**

Cold Hanworth Now converted into a house. It is a thousand pities that this important little church was not taken over by the Redundant Churches Fund. Now, fifteen years or so later, it would have been. By a little-known architect, J. Croft of Islington, it is High Victorian at its most exuberant. In a century or so it may be rescued, like the Saxon church at Bradford-on-Avon, which once suffered a similar fate.

Coleby The village tumbles over the side of the Cliff, and there are wide views to the west; the spire of the church presides over all. This is Perpendicular and crocketed, with small flying buttresses, but the tower itself is Saxon or early Norman; the south doorway is Norman, too, as are the north arcade and chancel arch; the south arcade is Early English, as is the chancel itself with its lancet windows. There are old bench-ends with poppyheads, and an elegant marble monument to Mary

Lister (1734). The Listers built the many-gabled Hall in the early seventeenth century: it passed by marriage to the Scropes, then to the Tempests of Broughton (Yorks). In the garden there is a grand temple of Romulus and Remus by Sir William Chambers (1762), and a smaller temple in honour of William Pitt.

Colsterworth A large village in the valley of the incipient River Witham, and famous as the birthplace of Sir Isaac Newton. Woolsthorpe Manor, where he was born on Christmas Day 1642, is a delightful seventeenth-century stone house, now the property of the National Trust and open to the public. The church where he was baptised has Norman and Transitional work, but is mostly Decorated and Perpendicular. The sundial cut by Newton when he was nine years old, and the register containing his baptism, are of special interest.

Coningsby Important Decorated and Perpendicular tower, with open ground floor for processions – and an enormous one-handed clock. Spacious church, all Decorated and Perpendicular; but the apsidal chancel is of 1874, by T. C. Hine of Nottingham.

Conisholme The village is on the main road; it is here that Applebys' celebrated ice creams are made: there is an ice cream parlour, with a car park opposite for visitors. The tiny church, fragment of a much larger building, is buried in back lanes in trees. There are blocked up Early English arcades, the head of an Anglo-Saxon cross with the figure of Christ, and a brass to John Langholme (1515) with his wife and fourteen children. A charming little church.

Corby Glen Once a small market town. The tower of the church stands prominent above the streets of stone houses, overlooking the upper River Glen. Apart from the Decorated north aisle all is Perpendicular, dignified and spacious. The important wall paintings were discovered in 1939, and date from the fourteenth century. There is an exquisite St Anne teaching the Virgin, a magnificent St Christopher, and a whole series of scenes of the Nativity, in addition to the more usual scenes of the Doom. They are the most extensive in the county. Delightful sixteenth/seventeenth-century rectory next door; the Old Grammar School, founded by Charles Read in 1673, is a distinguished and beautiful little building, now the Willoughby Memorial Gallery. There is a little Roman Catholic church (Our Lady of Mount Carmel), built here in 1855 with the materials of the old Roman Catholic chapel at Irnham Hall (*q.v.*).

Corringham An important Anglo-Saxon tower; inside, Norman and Early English arcades with Perpendicular clerestory – all splendidly restored and decorated by Bodley (1884): painted ceiling, rood screen, organ, chancel stalls; good Victorian glass by Wailes, Kempe and Powell; early nineteenth-century monuments to the Becketts of Somerby Park, Bodley's patrons.

Cotes-by-Stow A tiny church, Norman and later, far away in the fields to the east of Stow, among the outbuildings of a high-powered farm. It has much ancient woodwork: benchends, pulpit, remarkable traceried screen, complete with loft, approached by a stone staircase. Pearson restored the church tactfully in 1883, and there are brasses and small monuments in the chancel.

Covenham St Bartholomew and **Covenham St Mary** Between the Wolds and the coast – two churches but a stone's throw from one another. St Bartholomew's was ignominiously made redundant in 1981, and was threatened at one time with removal, stone by stone, to America. Now it has been saved by a private Trust, founded by John Bowles (Secretary of the Redundant Churches Fund), and is in process of restoration. It has an unusual low slate-hung central tower, nave, chancel and south transept, all Decorated – if somewhat Victorianised. It is hoped that its important Perpendicular font, transferred to a church in Manchester, and its notable early fifteenth-century brass to Sir John Skipwith – now in St Mary's – may be restored to the church.

St Mary's, nearby, is a charming Decorated church, with a white chalk tower and eighteenth-century porch, standing in a beautiful churchyard; a glistening interior, and another notable font.

Cowbit *(pronounced 'Cubbit')* A Perpendicular church of brick – with a stone tower – rises from *below* the road as it curves from Croyland to Spalding. The landscape is watered by the Welland and the New River, and was once famous for its skating championships, a scene reminiscent of a Breughel painting.

Cranwell Famous now for the RAF College, founded here in 1919. The buildings designed by Sir James Grey West are magnificent, and overlook enormous lawns, with long avenues and vistas. The poor village is sadly suburbanised: the little church by the green, with odd seventeenth-century bellcote and chancel higher than the nave, is in origin Saxon, and contains an important Norman arcade (with one capital of unusual ram's-head design). The pews were made from the panelling in the hall, a seventeenth-century Thorold mansion demolished in 1815.

Creeton looks blissful from the railway – the main Great Northern line – a little group of church, rectory, farmhouse on the hillside, with the ancient oaks of Grimsthorpe Park behind, and a scattering of small cottages at its feet. With its broach spire the church is chiefly late thirteenth century, but inside the chancel arch is twelfth century, and there are fragments of Anglo-Saxon cross shafts in the churchyard.

Croft One of the best of the Marshland churches, with tall tower, spacious, clerestoried nave, and large chancel – all Decorated and Perpendicular. But it is the fittings which make the church – a wealth of old

Croft

Runic Stone at Crowle (John Piper, Tate Archive). RIGHT *Croyland Abbey.*

woodwork, rood screen and parclose screens, seventeenth-century pulpit, medieval brass lectern. This was recovered from the moat of the old Hall, once the seat of the Browne family, to whom there are grand early seventeenth-century monuments. There is an early fourteenth-century brass with half effigy of a knight in chain-mail – one of the earliest brasses in England, and a monument to William Bonde (1559), erected by his son, President of Magdalen College, Oxford.

Crowle A decayed little town in the remote countryside of the Isle of Axholme. The churchyard is denuded of its headstones: a sad sight. The church is in origin Norman – but the nave arcade is Early English, and there has been much rebuilding in the eighteenth and again in the nineteenth century. An over-carpeted interior; the most interesting thing is the Runic Stone, which is perhaps tenth century, and carved with figures and dragons. Beautiful little Roman Catholic church of St Norbert, by M. E. Hadfield (1872).

Croxby A tiny hamlet in one of the prettiest valleys of the Wolds. There is a charming small mid-eighteenth-century Hall, and the diminutive church dates from the twelfth century. It looks nothing outside, but inside there is a Norman chancel arch, with the remains of a Norman south arcade; the blocked north arcade is thirteenth century. There is a Norman font, and bees nest in a crack of the wall outside.

Croxton The main road from Barrow to Brigg (A160), and a church with a many-pinnacled Perpendicular tower; the rest of the chuch (and indeed the base of the tower) is Decorated. Nothing special – but what is special is the panel of fourteenth-century glass of the Crucifixion in the south aisle.

Croyland is a strange, withdrawn little place, deep in the deepest Fens. Coming from the west, from civilisation, the long straight road accompanies the long straight canal-like River Welland for mile after straight mile, and eventually reaches the town. Like the hulk of an enormous wrecked ship, the remains of Cryland Abbey loom upon the horizon, and dominate the place. It is easy to imagine St Guthlac coming here in 669; a member of the Mercian royal house, and tired of soldiering, he retired to the monastery of Repton, and after two years of study resolved to become a hermit. He vowed that he would found his hermitage on whatever island in the swamps his boat first became stranded. Croyland was that place: it was St Bartholomew's Day 669. The Benedictine Abbey was founded here by King Ethelbald in 713 in his memory. After many ups and downs of fortune the Norman church was founded c. 1195, when the body of the saint was solemnly translated to the new church. There are remains of this Norman church, but what we see now is chiefly Early English and Perpendicular.

Approaching the church, the Early English west front is upon us, a west front of great beauty even in its fragmentary state. The doorway has in its tympanum a quatrefoil carved with scenes of the saint's life – including the day of his arrival here. On either side of the vast empty window (a Perpendicular insertion) is blind arcading adorned with canopied niches still containing original statues, all of great beauty, comparable with the west front of Wells. Through the doorway the nave is empty now, open to the sky, with fragments of the north arcade – which is Perpendicular – surviving, and the mammoth Norman chancel arch still standing above the pulpitum. Beyond there is nothing.

But to the north of the west front stands the enormous Perpendicular tower with its stunted spire, and the two-storeyed porch which leads into the surviving north aisle, now the parish church. It is a long, numinous, vaulted interior, with a screen (in part original) dividing nave from chancel, and a sanctuary lamp burning before the high altar. The deep bays on the north side contain chapels, or the organ. It is all cast in a dim religious light – but, turning west, the enormous windows under the tower make the whole west end a lantern of light. It is a haunting building.

In the centre of the town stands the triangular bridge – built in the fourteenth century to cross the Welland where three streams met. All are dry now. At the south-west approach there is a seated figure, perhaps of Christ, and perhaps the topmost figure of the west front, removed here in the eighteenth century.

Cumberworth At the back of beyond. At a leafy corner stands the church, a patchwork of brick and stone, partly medieval, partly nineteenth century, with an odd little lead-covered bell turret.

Cuxwold The Hall, surrounded by evergreen plantations, looks like an overgrown large Gothic house in North Oxford; it was built by Henry Thorold of Cuxwold in 1861 in polychromatic brick (J. K. Colling, architect). The little church has an early tower (Norman, or even Anglo-Saxon); the rest was much restored by James Fowler in 1860; Thorold monuments.

Dalby An undulating park, an early Victorian hall with bow windows and sashes; and a little church by James Fowler of 1862, containing two seventeenth-century monuments with kneeling figures, to the Llandon family.

Dawsmere One of the remote hamlets close to the Wash – charming, with trees and neat gardens, and enormous fields all round. The little apsidal church (1869) is very similar to Holbeach St Mark, and also by Ewan Christian – an intimate and religious building.

Deeping, Market see **Market Deeping**

Deeping, West see **West, Deeping**

Deeping St James A long street from Market Deeping, lined with stone cottages, and accompanied all the way by the River Welland; a church of unexpected size, with an early eighteenth-century tower and spire, and an array of large Decorated windows – but inside a great surprise: a long Transitional south arcade of such grandeur that Pevsner has described it as 'astounding'. This is the nave of the Benedictine priory, founded in 1139, botched up, knocked about, but magnificent.

Deeping St Nicholas In the middle of Deeping Fen: two big Georgian farmhouses, and a scattering of cottages – otherwise flat empty country-side, and a grand early Victorian church with prominent spire beside the main road. This is an early work by Charles Kirk (1845), in the Decorated style, with ample traceried windows, and is spacious, light and lofty; elaborate tomb, like an Easter sepulchre, to the founders, William and Nicholas Clarke Stevenson, by R. C. Hussey (1847).

Dembleby In a pretty valley off the Bridge End road; the tiny church has a genuine Norman chancel arch, and a very fine pillar piscina. The rest is a rebuilding by Charles Kirk in Norman Revival (1868).

Denton A stone village delightfully set against the plantations of its park, home of the Welbys. The church is spacious, with a tall Perpendicular tower, and an interior predominantly Perpendicular; monument to John Blyth (1602), and to Richard Welby (by Green of Camberwell, 1714), and many later memorials and hatchments; organ case by Bentley (1887).

Digby A good-looking church, with its Perpendicular crocketed spire and Perpendicular clerestoried nave; but the observant eye will soon notice that the lower part of the tower is Early English, and (if very observant) that there is Saxon long-and-short work at the south-east angle of the nave. The south doorway is indeed late Norman, and inside there are Early English and Decorated arcades – as well as old bench-ends and a Jacobean pulpit. Old village pound nearby, like a stone pepper pot.

Doddington Under the shadow the great house – a remarkable little church, a rebuilding of the medieval by William Lumby (1775). The details are so correct and convincing that it is difficult to believe that this is not the real thing. Only on the west tower Lumby had his fling; here is a delightful new doorway in Strawberry Hill Gothick, with doorway and niches on either side under gloriously carved and decorated ogee arches. Inside, a gallery of bright Victorian glass, a few box pews, a couple of hatchments. The house itself is always a thrill: built of pink brick and completed in 1600, it is almost certainly the work of Robert Smithson. With its gatehouse and lead cupolas, its walled gardens and gracious eighteenth-century interiors, it has descended from the builder through the Husseys and the Delavals to the Jarvis family, and is beautifully maintained, and open to the public on Wednesdays and Sundays in the summer.

Doddington, Dry see **Dry Doddington**

Donington A decayed but ancient little market town, with important Fen church, all Decorated and Perpendicular, with a grand south-west tower and spire crowning a spacious vaulted porch, and an interior a trifle prim with Victorian furnishings. Memorial to Matthew Flinders, the explorer (1814).

Donington-on-Bain Streams and stretches of water in a beautiful Wold valley, a rugged little church with an eleventh-century tower and a blocked thirteenth-century north arcade. An early seventeenth-century brass commemorates a former rector with these lines:

> Both Chrysostome and Polycarpe in one
> United lie interred beneath this stone
> This one a Phoenix was all eminent
> The learned prudent pious Thomas Kent

There is a Norman font, and an array of little holy pictures gives the interior an intimate cottagey atmosphere.

Dorrington The church stands on its own, half a mile from the village, on a low hill looking east across the Fens towards Tattershall: a severe tower, Transitional below, Decorated above, and the body of the church Decorated also, but for the Perpendicular nave clerestory. The most notable thing, easily missed, is the early fourteenth-century sculpture of the Doom, above the east window, outside.

Dowsby Slight Fen village with windbreak trees: the tall stone Elizabethan Hall, with gables and pinnacles, a big group of chimneys, and blind windows in the dormers, gazes out over the vast expanse of Fen to the east. The church has a Perpendicular tower, and Early English nave: the shaft of an Anglo-Saxon cross shaft is built into the east wall of the south aisle, outside.

Driby A remote and beautiful spot. The rolling wold, a handful of cottages and a farm, and the pretty little stone bell-turreted church of 1850. This has recently been turned into a private house, Driby St Michael – a tactful and delightful conversion by Francis Johnson; he has turned the upper part of the lofty nave into a wonderful airy solar.

Dry Doddington From its low hill there are astonishingly wide views – across the Valley of the Trent to the west, the Vale of Belvoir to the south, to Loveden Hill to the east, and (on a clear day) a glimpse of Lincoln Cathedral to the north. The church with its leaning broach spire (thirteenth-century) and Victorianised interior stands unfenced on its little green in the middle of the village: an endearing sight.

Dunholme A growing dormitory village, with an over-restored medieval church – Early English in origin, with bold west tower (with pinnacled Perpendicular top), a monument with kneeling figure to Robert Grantham (1618), and, preserved in a showcase, an interesting pre-Reformation leather satchel, for carrying the Blessed Sacrament.

Dunsby Small village in country of copses, close to the Fens. The

Leaning spire at Dry Doddington

Decorated tower of the church has in its second stage a figure of Our Lord under a crocketed gable (probably fourteenth century); Early English and Decorated nave and chancel, somewhat Victorianised; and noteworthy Perpendicular font with long inscription, hard to decipher in its mutilated state.

Dunston In the eighteenth century, before the enclosures, Dunston was a lonely village on the desolate Heath, a haunt of highwaymen: in 1751 Sir Francis Dashwood of West Wycombe who had come into the property in right of his wife, the widow of the last Ellys of Nocton (*q.v.*) erected the Dunston Pillar, surmounted by a lantern, 'the only land-lighthouse ever raised'. His successor in 1810 removed the lantern and, to celebrate George III's Jubilee, replaced it with a statue of the King (see Harmston). The pillar was monstrously reduced, as a danger to aircraft, in the Second World War; it is much to be hoped that it may yet be restored.

The small church was largely rebuilt by R. H. Carpenter in 1874.

Eagle From its low hill there is a wide view to the west across the valley of the Trent to the cooling towers at High Marnham. The little church has a low Early English tower, but with its wide overhanging eaves the rest is all of 1903, by J. T. Lee. 'To the glory of God, this stone was laid on the re-building of the church, the ancient possession of the Order of St John of Jerusalem, July 14th, 1903' reads an inscription in the east wall. There was once an important commandery of the Order here.

East Barkwith A Perpendicular tower with a seventeenth-century top, with straight-headed mullioned windows; a chancel of 1846 by J. B. Atkinson, and a north aisle by R. J. Withers. The rest is Perpendicular, with a Perpendicular porch with a small figure of the Virgin above the doorway. Inside, an ornate Perpendicular font, and an 'Arts and Crafts' pulpit by Christopher Turnor (of Stoke Rochford and Panton).

East Halton Only a mile from the Humber estuary: a scattered village against a background of angry-looking chimneys of the oil refineries on the coast. The church is chiefly Early English and Decorated, with triple lancets at the east end, and a solid tower; old benchends within.

East Keal Prominent at the extremity of the Wolds: the tower is of 1853, by Stephen Lewin, a good, original Victorian piece – and the rest of the church over-restored by him at this time; but the nave arcades are Early English, and there is a small Elizabethan monument with the seated figure of Susanna Kirkman, with her arm on a skull.

East Kirkby Where the Wolds slope down to the Fens. The church stands alone, its only companions a large brick Georgian farmhouse, a cottage, and the Victorian rectory. It is an important and beautiful building, with a south porch tower, vaulted, and Decorated nave and chancel – the chancel lofty with clerestory added by W. D. Caroe, who carried out an excellent restoration in 1906. Old pews, old screens, and an interesting assembly of fragments of (probably) an Easter sepulchre in the sanctuary.

East Ravendale One of James Fowler's happiest creations (1857): a lofty narrow nave, a lofty narrow chancel, impressive chancel arch, lancet windows everywhere. Moreover, there is a window by Burne-Jones (Morris & Co) of 1875, and another by Kempe (1882) – both of superb quality. Adjoining the church is the school, a delightful, asymmetrical, red brick Gothic building, also by Fowler.

East Stockwith On the east bank of the Trent, looking across to West Stockwith on the opposite bank (in Nottinghamshire). Little church by T. Johnson, by the waterside, built in 1846, with a bell turret – and a window by Wailes inside.

East Torrington A tiny village. The little church close to the Manor Farm is an attractive building by S.S. Teulon (1848), with Decorated features and pretty bellcote.

Eastville All on its own beside the long straight Fen road, a little group of church, school and vicarage by C. J. Carter (1840). More ambitious than most of these Fen chapels, with its pinnacled tower, apsidal chancel, and transepts, it is an interesting essay in primitive Perpendicular Revival.

Edenham A noble Perpendicular west tower, and a large and handsome church, Early English, Decorated and Perpendicular, noteworthy in itself, but doubly so on account of the wealth of magnifical monuments which it contains to the Dukes of Ancaster, Earls of Lindsey, Lords Willoughby de Eresby. There is the Restoration monument in the north chapel to Robert, 1st Earl of Lindsey and 12th Baron Willoughby de Eresby, and the breathtaking array in the chancel to the 1st, 2nd and 3rd and 4th Dukes, by Scheemakers and Cheere, Roubiliac (see over) and Charles Harris. These continue the series at Spilsby (*q.v.*).

Grimsthorpe Castle is nearby, part medieval, part Tudor, part Vanbrugh – and still the seat of the family.

Edlington A lodge at the top, on the main road from Lincoln to Horncastle, and an avenue down to the church, the site of the house, home of the Hassard-Shorts, and a handful of cottages. The church is of greenstone, with Perpendicular tower and thirteenth-century nave – but all restored and rebuilt by Fowler in 1860. Wide views across the Witham valley, to Lincoln in the far distance.

Elkington, North see **North Elkington**

Elkington, South see **South Elkington**

Elsham The slopes of the northernmost Wolds. The church stands above the village, heavily restored, almost rebuilt, by W. Scott Champion in 1874; but the Norman tower arch survives, together with other medieval parts. Elsham Hall is the home of the Elwes family, an eighteenth-century house splendidly added to in 1932 by Colonel Guy Elwes, the architect. There is a beautiful Roman Catholic Chapel.

Epworth 'I suppose you would call Epworth the Lourdes of Methodism' once declared the late Squire William Wright of Wold Newton, as he surveyed the Wesley Memorial Church here. John Wesley was born here in 1703, at the Old Rectory, which now belongs to the Methodist Church, and is open to the public; his father, Samuel Wesley, was rector here for thirty-nine years. The church is large, Early English and Decorated with a Perpendicular tower. Outside the chancel, on the south side, is the flat tomb of Samuel Wesley, from which his son preached on a visit to the place.

Evedon The little church with its squat tower appears to be slipping gently down the low hillside: it is of the thirteenth or early fourteenth century and contains a brass to Daniel Hardeby (1630), and a pretty marble monument to Sir Peregrine Bertie (1705).

Ewerby The tall, tapering broach spire rises majestically over plantations and flat fields: it is 172 feet high, and 'engaged' by the aisles. Ewerby is without question one of the most notable Decorated churches anywhere: it is all of a piece with flamboyant traceried windows and carved decoration everywhere. Grand pillars uphold the tower; there is no chancel arch – just a wide vista through rood screen or parclose screen to old woodwork or carved stonework everywhere. The nineteenth-century glass is good in itself, but too dark for the church, providing an over-dim religious light (which the Victorians loved).

Faldingworth twists and turns on the main road from Lincoln to Market Rasen: Hodgson Fowler's church and the Brownlow Arms are the landmarks. The former is of 1890, incorporating a few fragments of the medieval church, with a short shingled broach spire, like a village church in Surrey.

OPPOSITE *Edenham: monument to 2nd Duke of Ancaster by Roubiliac*

Farforth-cum-Maidenwell Glorious Wold country: tiny scattered community, with small bellcoted church of 1861.

Farlesthorpe A little village lost in the deepest Marsh, with a tiny church of brick and stone built in 1800, with a small chancel added in 1912 – and a large chicken farm for company.

Fenton A specially rewarding little church in a farmyard, next to the remains of the Old Hall (1597), burnt at the end of the eighteenth century and patched up, once the home of the Lucas family: Sir Gervase Lucas, Royalist Governor of Belvoir Castle, was created a baronet in 1644. The crocketed spire is distinguished Perpendicular work, and much resembles Claypole next door (*q.v.*); the old lead roof of the nave and the south aisle is a wonderful sight – 'looking like wet sheets left out to dry'. Inside, a Norman north arcade, old roofs, Perpendicular screens and pulpit, and a splendid set of pews with poppyheads, some original, some excellent nineteenth-century copies, create a picture of delightful rustic charm. This forgotten church was saved from dereliction a few years ago, thanks to the Lincolnshire Old Churches Trust and other friends.

Ferriby, South see **South Ferriby**

Fillingham On the Cliff above the village stands Fillingham Castle, or Summer Castle as it was called in the eighteenth century, a castellated Gothic house with round towers at the corners, built in 1760 for Sir Cecil Wray, perhaps by Carr of York. There are fine views from here across the lake below, called Fillingham Broad, and the flat lands to the west. The village nestles round the church – an odd patchwork of a building, medieval in origin, but Georgianised in the eighteenth century when the thirteenth-century arcades were filled in; the tower, open at its base to north, south and west, is of 1777.

Firsby Firsby Junction, on the line from Peterborough to Louth and Grimsby, traversing mile after endless mile of Fen and Marsh, is no more, its handsome station laid low. The church (to the south) is by G. E. Street (1856), attractive, bellcoted and apsed, unmistakably the work of the great man.

Fishtoft A vegetable village near Boston, close to the seabank of the Wash. A scatter of farms, and a big Fenland church, externally all Perpendicular, with a plain embattled tower, and, inside, earlier arcades, ancient screens, old pulpit.

Fenton and (right) Fillingham (John Piper, Tate Archive). BELOW *Fishtoft (John Piper, Tate Archive).*

Fiskerton The back road from Lincoln to Bardney, close to the Witham: there are views from here which de Wint loved to paint. The church has a pinnacled Perpendicular tower, and lofty clerestoried nave, but inside the north arcade is Norman, the south Early English, and there is a Norman arcade in the chancel – it is, in fact, a very early church, with the remains of an early round tower enclosed in the present tower. Old benchends; fifteenth-century brass of a priest, rescued from a dealer's shop in Lincoln.

Fleet A special pleasure and surprise: a church with a detached spire – indeed a tower and spire of noble Decorated grandeur. The nave is spacious, with wide aisles separated by Early English arcades; everywhere there are windows with Decorated tracery, but the great west window is Perpendicular.

Flixborough Despite the proximity of Scunthorpe and industry, an attractive stone-built village: little church of 1886 by Hodgson Fowler, with a shingled bellcote.

Folkingham One of the great pleasures of Lincolnshire – to drive slowly up the hillside, and arrive in the wide Market Place face to face with the splendid eighteenth-century façade of the Greyhound, other charming houses all around, and the House of Correction (now Landmark Trust) along the lane to Billingborough. The church stands up an alley in the north-west corner of the Market Place, with its lofty Perpendicular tower crowned with many pinnacles, its vaulted porch of two storeys, and its Perpendicular rood screen.

Fosdyke A very red red-brick church by Browning (1871), with a broach spire of lead, and a handsome well-proportioned interior. Iron bridge over the Welland, busy with small craft.

Foston A homely village, by-passed by the A1, surveying the Nottinghamshire borderlands from its low hill. The church with its Early English tower presides; inside, Early English arcades with a diminutive clerestory, and a narrow Norman chancel arch.

Fotherby Traffic rushes past along the main road from Louth to Grimsby: James Fowler's church (1863) presides over the village. Its broach spire, from a distance, might pass for a medieval building, but at close quarters its Victorian details stand out. As a Victorian building it is impressive; inside, red brick, it is colourful and warm.

Frampton The ugly suburban growth along the main road is depressing – but the old village is a charming oasis, with many pretty cottages,

Folkingham: the church from the Market Place

and an early eighteenth-century Hall, with stables and wrought-iron screens – curiously Jacobethanised in the nineteenth century; it was the home of the Tunnards and Tunnard-Moores. The church has a great solid Transitional tower, crowned with an Early English broach spire. A long, dark, mysterious interior, Early English and Decorated, with a splendid eighteenth-century brass candelabrum, and monuments to the Tunnards.

There is a small church at West Frampton by James Fowler (1863), stone and brick, attractive with its modest bellcote.

Freiston A sea-girt parish, close to the Wash, and the grand fragment of a Benedictine priory, founded in 1114. A wonderful multi-coloured, multi-textured exterior of stone and brick, all apparently Perpendicular, with severe west tower – but inside there is a long Norman nave, extended to the west in the thirteenth century. The east end is blocked – crossing and monastic choir were demolished at the Dissolution – but there are old screens to the chapels, and the octagonal fifteenth-century font is crowned with its original canopied cover. A most rewarding church.

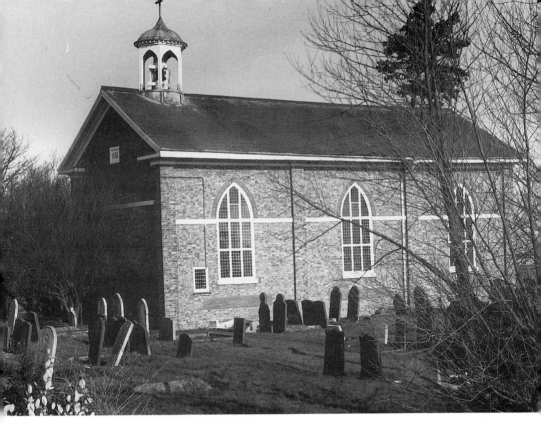

Frithville: one of Jephtha Pacey's Fen chapels

Friesthorpe An unassuming little church of 1841, attached to a mediev-al tower: lancet windows, everything basic – but a white-painted glistening interior, with painted pews and clear glass windows: just the way to treat a little church like this.

Friskney A large straggling village, just off the main coast road from Boston to Wainfleet (A52). Delightful eighteenth-century rectory, to the west of the church. This is one of the great churches of the Marsh: the base of the tower is Norman, the lower stages Early English, but the top is Perpendicular, as indeed is most of the church, with its spacious clerestoried nave and chancel. There are Perpendicular screens, a Jaco-bean pulpit, somewhat faded fourteenth-century wall paintings in the nave clerestory, huge Victorian framed pictures, and an east window by Wailes (1850).

Frithville One of Jephtha Pacey's little brick Fen chapels, sitting char-mingly at the intersection of several roads: a small Classical cupola, a pedimented west front with the date 1821 firmly in the centre, and simple traceried Gothic side windows.

Fulbeck One of the prettiest villages in the county, with lanes descending the valley, and many good houses: the Manor has gables of golden stone and sloping lawns, Fulbeck House a handsome early eighteenth-century front; pride of place must go to the Hall (1733), approached by its lime avenue and splendid eighteenth-century gates surmounted by the arms of the Fanes, who still live here. Next door is the church with its distinguished lofty Perpendicular tower, and Perpendicular clerestoried nave; inside there are earlier arcades, and, everywhere, monuments to the Fanes. Of special charm is the one to Thomas Bell: 'He was for fifty years a faithful servant to Sir Francis Fane, Knt of ye Bath ... and travelled with him into Holland, Denmark, Germany, Loraine, Switzerland, Italy, Naples, France and Flanders, where hee considered ye courts and camps of most of ye European princes, their splendor and mutabilitie, concluding with ye preacher there was nothing new under the sun and yt all was vanity and onely one thing necessary, to fear God and keep his commandments. Soe doth F. F. who fixed this stone 1674.'

Fulletby A particularly beautiful spot, with wide views across the Wolds to Somersby and the Tennyson Valley. A modest little church, almost entirely rebuilt by Fowler in 1857, of greenstone and bellcoted, but containing a genuine Decorated sedilia.

Fulstow In the Marsh, between the A16 and the coast. The church was largely rebuilt in 1868, but an Early English south doorway remains, with fragments of the Early English arcades. There are fourteenth-century effigies in the porch, and an Early English font. (See Introduction).

Gainsborough It is always interesting to visit this rather odd, detached, little industrial town on the Trent. Dreary red houses line the approaches, and the narrow streets leading to the centre are made up of forbidding factories or gloomy warehouses. But along the river bank are the quays where, as George Eliot has described them in *The Mill on the Floss*, 'black ships laden with fresh-scented fir planks, with rounded sacks of oil-bearing seed, or with the dark glitter of coal' have always tied up; and the big warehouses where the imports to this inland port are housed. And exploring the narrow streets in this part of the town, the visitor, almost by accident, will suddenly espy the Tudor chimneys and towers of the Old Hall, one of the most important surviving ancient houses in England, sitting on a drab patch of grass, surrounded by depressing semi-detached villas. This grand fifteenth-century manor house, built of brick and timber (only the oriel window of the Great Hall

Gainsborough: the interior of All Saints

in stone), was in turn the seat of the Lords Burgh, then the Hickmans, in origin London merchants (but related to the Burghs), before they removed to the 'sylvan pleasances' of Thonock outside the town. In the course of the next century or two different parts of it were used as a linen factory, a theatre, a Congregational chapel, a public house, a corn exchange, and a block of tenements: its survival seems incredible. All the Hickman property descended to the Bacons (premier baronets of England) and in 1952 Sir Edmund Bacon leased it at a peppercorn rent to the Friends of the Old Hall Association, who began repairs. It is now administered by the County Council, and open to the public.

It is also a great pleasure to visit the parish church, so different in date and style, built between 1736 and 1744 by Francis Smith of Warwick, and attached to the Perpendicular tower of the old church. It is a wonderful, spacious Classical interior, with galleries and Corinthian

Gainsborough: All Saints. RIGHT *Gautby: Sir Thomas Vyner.*

columns. There is an incongruous but beautiful pulpit by Pearson (1869), and some good Victorian glass including one window (north aisle) designed by Bodley.

Holy Trinity, a thin Gothic building by J. Johnson (1849), is now deconsecrated and used as the 'Trinity Centre' – a theatre and exhibition hall – and St John the Divine, by Micklethwaite and Somers Clark (1882), alas never completed, is but an embryo of the great church originally planned.

Garthorpe On the west side of the Trent, close to its junction with the Ouse: a little red brick church of 1913, by Wilfrid Bond.

Gate Burton A small church of 1866, with Decorated details and a pinnacled tower, on the edge of the park of Gate Burton Hall. A beautiful interior with Norman font, and a spacious, devotional sanctuary with effective altar and reredos of c. 1930. The south front of the Hall is a plain eighteenth-century building of white brick (built by the Huttons), the north front is in red brick, of 1913 by Detmar Blow, grandly Baroque à la Wren; in the park, on the far side of the main road, is a delectable little mid-eighteenth-century folly, a prospect house to enjoy the views of the Trent – known as the 'Burton Shatoo' (château); it is now the property of the Landmark Trust.

Gautby No man's land – between Bardney and Horncastle, and all the atmosphere of a long-lost great house: crumbling brick walls enclosing forgotten gardens, a surviving stable block, a mutilated park, a lake largely silted up. Gautby Hall of the Vyners was pulled down but their charming little Georgian brick church (1756 – much the same date as the house) survives, with its tower and short lead spire, Venetian east window, and grand chancel arch with Ionic pilasters. There are two seventeenth-century monuments with reclining figures, removed from St Mary Woolnoth (London EC3), and many ledger stones in the sanctuary. A beautifully furnished, atmospheric little church.

Gayton-le-Marsh A Perpendicular greenstone tower, and a Victorian red brick church were conveniently condemned as 'dangerous' twenty odd years ago, and demolished. In the end, dynamite was needed. Dangerous? A shameful business.

Gayton-le-Wold A modest, unassuming, little red brick Victorian church, in a tree-lined churchyard in wonderful Wold country near Louth.

Gedney In the Fens the churches sail past like ships at sea; Gedney is one of the grandest of these. As the church sails into view the transparency of its great plain glass windows, and its tall clerestory of twelve paired lights, cannot fail to thrill the passing traveller. And the scale of everything is breathtaking. The lofty tower was built in three stages, beginning with Early English and ending in Perpendicular. The interior is somewhat mutilated, but has a threadbare beauty and spaciousness. Important remains of fourteenth-century Jesse window, and other considerable remains of medieval glass; seventeenth-century pulpit, seventeenth-century Welby monuments.

Gedney Hill Hill? – a barely perceptible rise of ground. The church is Perpendicular, with an embattled tower – somewhat rebuilt by James Fowler in 1875. The most interesting feature is the unusual massive oak medieval pillars to the nave arcade.

Glentham The church stands forlornly in a churchyard denuded of its tombs and headstones – a miserable sight. There is an eighteenth-century tower, and an attractive wide Perpendicular porch, with a *pieta* above the entrance, and the arms of the Tournays who lived at Caenby (*q.v.*). Spacious Perpendicular interior, with box pews, two Tournay tombs, and a window by Christopher Whall (1915).

Glentworth An early Norman (or late Saxon) tower, an eighteenth-century nave, and a medieval chancel. In the chancel is the magnificent tomb of Sir Christopher Wray, Queen Elizabeth's Lord Chief Justice,

Gedney and (right) Gosberton spire

and Speaker of the House of Commons (d. 1592); opposite, the white marble monument of Elizabeth Sanderson, by Edward Hurst (1714). The Sandersons, Earls of Castleton, inherited the Wray property here, and it subsequently descended to the Lumleys, Earls of Scarbrough. The Hall was built by James Paine for the 4th Earl of Scarbrough in 1713 – on to a fragment of Sir Christopher's Tudor house; it is now ruinous, and looks like a phantom from the hillside above.

Goltho A tiny church, of Tudor brick, among trees – just visible from the main road from Lincoln to Wragby – in a field made bumpy with the foundations of a great house, once the seat of the Grantham family. A little nave, with mullioned windows of brick, and a slightly later chancel, once with an oval window – but blocked when the handsome early eighteenth-century reredos was installed. With its eighteenth-century Communion rails, two-decker pulpit, and box pews, this was all reopened with a flourish some years ago – but then once more given over to cows and crows. Disgraceful. But now it is in the loving hands of the Redundant Churches Fund, and in the process of restoration. *Laus Deo*. A precious little building.

Gosberton A Fen village, where busy roads meet: cottages of warm red brick line the streets, and there are one or two larger houses – such as Gosberton House, three storeys high with pediment and small cupola (now a school). The church is one of great magnificence, Decorated and Perpendicular, cruciform with central tower and crocketed spire, grand transepts, traceried windows and a spacious and many-vistaed interior.

At Gosberton Clough, on the long Fen road, two miles to the west, is a tiny church of 1902 by Comper, of timber and plaster, delightful with its Comper windows and furnishing.

Goulceby Wold village, in superbly beautiful, remote countryside. The little church with its bellcote is chiefly a rebuilding of 1908, but using the old materials of its predecessor.

Goxhill A grand pinnacled Perpendicular tower to dominate the flat Humber landscape, and a church with an imposing clerestoried Perpendicular nave, and earlier chancel. Mural painting of the Crucifixion with attendant figures (fifteenth century); seventeenth-century pulpit.

To the south, across the railway, is a building often called the Priory – which it never was; it is in fact the Great Hall (fourteenth century) of a medieval house, standing on a vaulted undercroft, with a handsome early eighteenth-century brick house adjoining.

Grainsby A charming backwater, and a very pretty church, largely unrestored, with Early English tower and other medieval features, but with eighteenth-century brick patchwork, and domestic-looking windows, and a simple Perpendicular chancel screen inside. The park is delightful: the Victorian Hall has gone, but the Haigh family still live in a smaller house; avenues of black poplars give the setting a French feel.

Grainthorpe A handsome church with imposing Perpendicular tower – the rest Decorated or Perpendicular with Decorated traceried windows; those in the chancel are specially delightful. Beautiful ogee arch to north door, and a spacious wide Marshland interior, with old roofs and old brick floors. A wonderful solitary spot.

Grantham celebrated its quincentenary as a borough in 1963, and this ushered in a programme of wholesale butchery of some of its best eighteenth-century streets. It is hard to conceive how such destruction could have been countenanced: High Street, Watergate and Vine Street have all suffered: in Watergate one whole side of the street has been replaced by a miserable car park; in Vine Street the mysterious narrow winding entry, leading to the parish church, has gone; in High Street

OPPOSITE *Grantham spire, according to Sir George Gilbert Scott, 'second only to Salisbury in beauty'*

the sacrifice of decent Georgian houses continues, with the recent destruction of Waterloo House, and its replacement by a barbarous block entirely unsuited to a country town. Mercifully, the celebrated medieval Angel Hotel and the handsome eighteenth-century George have been allowed to survive – but in the case of the George only just.

Round the parish church some dignity remains: on the north side stands the eighteenth-century vicarage, with the sixteenth-century King's School next door – like the quadrangle of a small Oxford college; to the east is Grantham House – originally fourteenth century, and the home of the Hall family, it was refronted in Georgian times. It now belongs to the National Trust.

It is a great experience to approach the west front of the church – as distinguished as that of any parish church in England. Here Ruskin stood spellbound. Above soars the spire, 281 feet high, built between 1280 and 1300 – before Salisbury (404 feet), before Norwich (345 feet), before Coventry (300 feet), before Louth (294 feet). In its day it was the tallest spire in the country – the first of the great spires of England. Notice the 'engaged' aisles, and two of the enormous geometrical windows: on walking round, the remarkable series of wonderful traceried windows continues. Inside, the columns on which the tower stands are awe-inspiring; the nave arcades (early thirteenth century) will also impress. The church is enormously wide, with aisles almost as broad as the nave: the power of this grand interior is horizontal rather than vertical. Most of the furnishings are by Gilbert Scott, but the splendid reredos is by Sir Arthur Blomfield. There is a varied and interesting collection of monuments. Beneath the Lady Chapel is a vaulted crypt.

St John's, near the railway station, is by Salvin (1840), and St Anne's by Bertram Tarrant (1906); St Mary's (RC), a chaste little Classical building by E. J. Willson (1832), has been enlarged by a wide extension on the north side.

Grasby The main road from Caistor to Brigg runs along the top of the Wold: Grasby lies on the hillside below. Charles Tennyson-Turner, the poet's brother, came to be rector here in 1837, and stayed for forty years; he was himself a poet. The tower and nave arcades are thirteenth century, but there was much rebuilding in 1869. Tennyson memorials.

Grayingham A plump, stocky medieval tower – the rest plain Georgian (1773), but Victorianised by James Fowler a century later. A forlorn little village in obscure country near Kirton Lindsey.

Great Carlton A pretty, leafy village, on the edge of the Marsh. The church is an ambitious rebuilding by James Fowler (1860) in the Decorated style, with a (genuine) Perpendicular west tower.

Great Coates Dangerously close to Grimsby, but still retaining some village character: an interesting church with an early nave (Early English arcades with clustered columns, but round arches), Decorated chancel, Perpendicular tower. There are two brasses, one to Isabella, wife of Roger Barnardiston (c. 1420), the other to Sir Thomas (1503), members of the ancient Suffolk family, who acquired this manor by marriage with a Willoughby heiress in the fourteenth century.

Great Gonerby The village is by-passed now (by the A1) – so it is possible to stand and admire the church, externally all of a piece with its Perpendicular spire, clerestory, parapet and pinnacles; all distinguished work. Inside there is an Early English south arcade, and the aisle windows are Decorated. Grand views from the hillside.

Great Grimsby Grimsby is an ancient port and borough, which over the centuries has had its ups and downs of fortune. It was the coming of the Great Central Railway in the middle of the nineteenth century which changed all this: new fish docks were built, and the fishing industry which had languished in the seventeenth and early eighteenth centuries revived. New graving docks were built, new shipbuilding and engineering works established – and the population of fish and men leapt astronomically.

But Grimsby is a poor town to look at. The population rose so rapidly that there seems to have been no time to plan: there are long featureless streets, with hardly a building of any consequence. There were a number of Victorian and Edwardian churches; many of these have gone, whether welcome victims of road-widening schemes, or conveniently condemned as 'unsafe' buildings. The most exciting building in the town is undoubtedly the Dock Tower (1852) – in fact a hydraulic tower – which rises above the docks like the tower of Siena Town Hall. It was designed by J. W. Wild.

St James's (the parish church) is a grand medieval building, and the ancient mother church of Grimsby, spectacular proof of the importance of the place in the Middle Ages. It is a big cruciform building, with central tower, nave of six bays, transepts, dignified chancel – all early thirteenth century in date. Long lancets adorn the east end, the clerestory in the nave is, as it were, triforium and clerestory combined: a very effective arrangement. The Lady Chapel (north transept) is by Bodley (1906), the Chapel of the Resurrection by Sir Charles Nicholson (1920).

Great Grimsby: the interior of St Augustine's

The church was bombed during the Second World War, and there has been much sympathetic restoration; all the same, the building has lost some of its ancient texture.

Of the other churches, St Augustine's is a lovely church by Sir Charles Nicholson (1911). Outwardly it is a large but undistinguished brick building: inside, with its wide nave and wide aisles, whitewashed, with Nicholson's own free Gothic details, it is a building of real atmosphere. Charmingly furnished with pews painted green, and rood screen, it glows with flickering sanctuary lamps and votive candles – the kind of church that compels one to one's knees.

St Martin's (1937) is a successful church by Lawrence Bond, well-proportioned and articulate; St Mark's (1960) by Vernon Royle, with its cubic forms and oddly shaped tower, is very much a product of the '60s. It is spacious, but somehow lacking in atmosphere – not the fault of the architect.

All Saints' is a large, somewhat bleak building by J. F. K. and S. P.

Cutts (1904), with some glass by Burlison and Grylls – closed, although surrounded by a large and otherwise churchless parish. No doubt it will be pulled down: a defeatist policy.

Already St Andrew's (by J. H. Hakewill, 1870) has been demolished; St Stephen's, a distinguished building by Sir Walter Tapper (1914), and St Luke's, a beautiful church by Sir Charles Nicholson (1912), built as a memorial to Bishop King, and St Paul's West Marsh (by R. J. Withers, 1868) have gone: a highly successful purge. It is very sad, and no credit to the Diocese of Lincoln.

(See also Cleethorpes, Old Clee, Humberston, and Scartho.)

Great Hale The church lost its chancel in the Civil War, but the Early English nave of five lofty bays is impressive, as is the great late Saxon (or early Norman) tower, crowned with Perpendicular pinnacles. There are two small seventeenth-century monuments to the Cawdron family, with kneeling figures.

Great Humby is much smaller than Little Humby – just a solid farm-house, and a scattering of cottages. The precious little church is that rare thing, a seventeenth-century chapel, sitting on a grass plot with a pond

Great Humby

nearby. It was originally the private chapel of the long lost Humby Hall, the Brownlow home before Belton was built; when they migrated, the chapel was left to serve the parish. It was built in 1682. It is tiny: a bellcote, a four-centred arched doorway, mullioned windows. It was saved from dereliction in the late 1970s, thanks to the Lincolnshire Old Churches Trust and other friends, and is vested in the Trust and used regularly for Sunday worship.

Great Limber An attractive village with pond and willows, and many estate cottages. A spacious church, mostly Early English and Decorated, with solid square tower, and long nave with wide aisles, rood screen and Victorian furnishings.

Nearby on a tumulus among cedar trees stands the Brocklesby Mausoleum, built by James Wyatt, 1787-94, in memory of Sophia, wife of the 1st Lord Yarborough. Domed and colonnaded, the centre of the dome is glazed – with glass painted with angels' heads and clouds by Francis Eginton: below stands Nollekens's figure of Sophia; around stand other sculptured groups of the family. It is James Wyatt's masterpiece.

Great Ponton The tower of silvery stone, built in 1519 by Anthony Ellys, merchant of the staple in Calais, is a wonderful sight from the Great North Road – or from the railway line to the east, presiding over its village, with the infant River Witham flowing in the valley below. The church itself, mostly Perpendicular, is on an altogether smaller scale, but next door is Anthony Ellys's beautiful little stone manor house, with crow-stepped gables and mullioned windows. Inside, on the first floor, there are contemporary wall paintings.

Great Steeping Take the lane marked NO THROUGH ROAD, on and on between thick hedges, and across the track of an extinct railway – and at the end stands a little brick church of 1748, with stone dressings and a small bell turret. It is a delightful little building, now in the care of the Redundant Churches Fund.

The 'new' church stands in the village, and is built of flaming red brick (1891), W. Bassett Smith, architect.

Great Sturton Departed glory: the great medieval house of the Clintons stood here, the site now marked by grassy moats; the Victorian mansion of the Liveseys has likewise disappeared. The church is a fragment, with Norman door, Decorated chancel, medieval wall painting, royal arms of George III, and splendid timbers to support the belfry – all delightfully rehabilitated by Micklethwaite in 1904.

Great Ponton: 'the tower of silvery stone'

Greatford A very pretty spot, with stone cottages and the little River Glen running by. The church is a distinguished building of the Early English and Decorated periods, with a broach spire unusually placed above the south transept. Of special interest is the piscina in the north transept, placed in the squint, its bowl adorned with six beautifully carved oak leaves surrounding the drain. Nearby, again of great interest, is the marble monument by Nollekens to the Revd Francis Willis, MD, who cured George III's insanity. He died in 1807. He and his son had an asylum for 'afflicted persons of distinction and respectability' at the Hall, the Elizabethan house next to the church.

Greetwell Ancient church and ancient Hall, across a small bumpy park; the church has an early tower, a Norman chancel arch and apse – all carefully restored by Hodgson Fowler in 1899. There are a few interesting monuments, especially one to Richard Lely, 'Petri Lely, Car. II Pictoris Nepos Natu-maximus' (1736), and a little organ in a pretty painted case. The Hall, once the home of Dalisons and Lelys, is a patched-up Jacobean house – and with the church forms a delightful group.

Grimoldby A large greenstone church of Marshland character, all late fourteenth century, with tall tower, and wide clerestoried nave. Inside, Perpendicular screen, partly original, and a number of old benches.

Grimsby, Great see **Great Grimsby**

Grimsby, Little see **Little Grimsby**

Gunby St Nicholas A little stone village close to the Rutland border: the small church, of which only the tower is old, was rebuilt in 1869 (see Stainby), and is filled with the carvings of a former rector, W. A. H. Thorold.

Gunby St Peter Famous for Gunby Hall, the William and Mary house built by Sir William Massingberd, 2nd baronet, in 1700. Of plum-coloured brick with stone dressings, three storeys high, it stands like a lovable big dolls' house, surrounded by exquisite gardens, Tennyson's 'haunt of ancient peace'. It was given to the National Trust by Field-Marshal Sir Archibald Montgomery-Massingberd, former CIGS, and his wife in 1944.

The little church on the edge of the garden is by James Fowler (1868), and contains two important brasses, one to Sir Thomas Massingberd (1552) – though dating from a century earlier – the other to William Lodynton (1420).

Gunness The village has grown up round Keadby Bridge, which was opened in 1916 – the King George V Bridge, as it is properly called – and provides the only access (road and rail) with the isle of Axholme, that forgotten part of Lincolnshire. There is a small post-war brick church (by Haynes and Johnson of Brigg) in Gunness, or Gunhouse, as the old name was.

Habrough The railway line from Barnetby to Grimsby makes a long loop to avoid Brocklesby. There is a grand railway station. The straggling village of Habrough is beyond, with a small stone church of 1869 by R. J. Withers, with a little octagonal tower and spire.

Hacconby A busy farming village, looking out across the Fens; the most notable feature of the church is the robust early fourteenth-century tower, built of alternate courses of ashlar and ironstone, with a plain parapet, then a tapering recessed spire, with pinnacles hugging its base. The body of the church is earlier (thirteenth century), with a Perpendicular clerestory, and there is a Perpendicular north-east chapel, a distinguished little building. A spacious interior, and, although scraped, not lacking in atmosphere.

Haceby A tiny, almost deserted village, in the inconsequential lanes which run criss-cross over the unfrequented countryside of the Stone Belt. A church with a solid tower – Norman in its base, Decorated in its upper stages; a Perpendicular arcade, a south aisle and clerestory, and an Early English chancel with a seventeenth-century east window. Over the narrow early Norman chancel arch the seventeenth-century royal arms has recently been uncovered and restored. A homely, devout little church, now in the care of the Redundant Churches Fund.

Hackthorn Church and Hall make a perfect picture across the Park. The Hall was built for John Cracroft (his descendants still live here) by James Lewis in 1792; the church in 1850 at the expense of (and probably to the design of) Charles Mainwaring, who was at that time lay rector. In feeling, and in its furnishings, it seems a decade or two earlier than 1850. The tower is supposedly a slightly cut-down version of Magdalen tower, and most of the details of the building are Perpendicular inside, the furnishings are eloquent of William IV rather than of Victoria – especially the Cracrofts' pew in the gallery. (The full story of the furnishings is told in the *Shell Guide*). There is good nineteenth-century glass – the east window by Wailes, the chancel south window by Holiday. All this, and a number of family monuments, will bring great pleasure to every visitor.

Hagnaby (*near Spilsby*) 'SAINT ANDREW' proclaims the iron gate to the churchyard – but even this is padlocked. It is just possible to peer through and see the pretty little Georgian church (with some Victorian glorifications) standing among the yews and hollies, almost in the garden of what remains of Charles Kirk's big Tudor Gothic house of 1835 – misleadingly called Hagnaby Priory. (For Hagnaby Priory proper see Hannah.)

Hagworthingham The tower collapsed in 1975: the church itself survives, a medieval church drastically restored by James Fowler in 1859. It is his strong Victorian spirit which possesses the place; east window by Wailes.

Hainton The road from Wragby to Louth skirts the park, landscaped by Capability Brown in 1763: the Hall, where the Heneages have lived since the fourteenth century, and still live, is visible through the trees; in origin it is their Tudor house, and what must have been the Great Hall was in the eighteenth century converted into a magnificent two-storeyed room, adorned with Ionic pilasters and handsome plasterwork – and there are other delightful Georgian rooms. The spire of the church rises behind the house – built apparently at Capability's suggestion to provide an eye-catcher across the park. The church was considerably rebuilt in 1848 by E. J. Willson, but contains a remarkable collection of family monuments from 1435 to the present time. From the brass to John Heneage in the floor of the Heneage Chapel (1435), and the brass to another John set in its Purbeck marble tomb in the chancel (1530), the sequence is continuous. There are kneeling figures facing each other across a prayer desk, a recumbent effigy in alabaster, a garlanded monument of the late seventeenth century, sophisticated tablets of the eighteenth and nineteenth centuries – the older monuments all glowing with gilt and colour. The Heneages continued Papist right through the penal times, and there is a Catholic church in the garden, also by E. J. Willson (1836) in Gothic brick. Willson (himself a Catholic) is buried in the churchyard.

Hale, Great see **Great Hale**

Haltham-on-Bain In the quiet meadows of the Bain, a little church of greenstone patched with brick, with humble wooden belfry and noble east window of flowing tracery. A wonderful interior, with old pews in various directions facing a two-decker pulpit, a medieval chancel screen, and a parclose on the north side rearranged at some time to enclose a family pew. There are old floors, old tiles, old prayer books, a

The Heneage Chapel at Hainton

Haltham: 'in the quiet meadows of the Bain'

royal arms of Charles I, and a visitors' book of 1898. Now in the care of the Redundant Churches Fund.

Halton, East see **East Halton**

Halton, West see **West Halton**

Halton Holgate A delightful spot on the very edge of the Wolds: from the churchyard there are wonderful views across the Fens. The church is of considerable magnificence, almost entirely Perpendicular with a grand tower, clerestoried nave, and spacious interior. Old roofs with angels, and a wealth of old woodwork (choir stalls, benchends) make this a most rewarding church.

Hameringham The southern slopes of the Wolds as they gently descend towards Revesby. The little church fell down, and was rebuilt by Hodgson Fowler in 1893, using the old stones and incorporating the

Corbel heads at Haltham-on-Bain. RIGHT *Halton Holgate.*

Early English nave arcade. It is an attractive little building of greenstone, with a wooden bellcote.

Hannah An unsophisticated little eighteenth-century church of greenstone, standing on a little knoll not far from the coast, in Marshland; a delightful interior, complete with box pews, two-decker pulpit, and

Hannah: country Georgian

Hannah: the interior. RIGHT *Harmston: monument to Sir George Thorold.*

Georgian altar rails. Some twelfth-century fragments in the porch, from Hagnaby Priory, the Premonstratensian house founded in 1175 – whose site (to the west) is occupied by Abbey Farm.

Hareby There is really very little of Hareby – just Hareby House, a cottage or so, and a minute church; but the view across the southern slopes of the Wolds towards the fens is a delight. The church is of greenstone and brick, largely of 1858, but incorporating fragments from the earlier church – such as the charming little fourteenth-century niche above the west door.

Harlaxton Harlaxton Manor is unquestionably one of the greatest nineteenth-century houses in England – built between 1831 and 1837 for George de Ligne Gregory by Salvin and Burn. Stand at the top of the drive, under the arch on the main road, and gaze down the long drive, across the bridge, through the gatehouse, on and up to the mansion sitting above and nestling in the hillside. The house is huge, and the whole composition Vanbrughesque in proportion and detail – but it is Vanbrugh translated into Jacobethan revival. The incredible interiors – especially the staircase – are decorated in exuberant, extravagant Baroque, providing a visitor ascending from front door to Long Gallery with a bewildering theatrical experience. The house is now the European campus of the University of Evansville, and splendidly cared for.

The church is large and handsome with tall tower and spire – externally all Perpendicular, except for the lower stages of the tower; there is earlier work within, and an interesting array of de Ligne and Gregory monuments and hatchments.

Harmston A grand Norman tower with Perpendicular pinnacled top, an impressive and elaborate Norman arch into the nave, and an Anglo-Saxon cross shaft with a representation of the Crucifixion at its head – these are relics of early days. The church otherwise is by Withers (1868), to replace the church built by Sir George Thorold in 1717 (see the inscription on the magnificent royal arms). There are monuments to Sir George (1722) and Sir Samuel (1738), with busts; under the tower is the ledger stone to Samuel Thorold (1820), illegitimate son of Sir Nathaniel Thorold, the last baronet of Harmston, who lived and died in the isle of Capri: the full, entertaining story is told in James Money's *Capri, Island of Pleasure* (Hamish Hamilton, 1986). In the churchyard is the headstone to John Willson, who fell from Dunston Pillar while erecting the statue of George III (1810):

> He who erected the noble king
> Is here now laid by death's sharp sting.

Harmston Hall, built by Sir George Thorold in 1710, but much enlarged and now a hospital, surveys the grand view from its terrace.

Harpswell The church sits squat under the Cliff: the tower is Anglo-Saxon, the nave arcade thirteenth century – a spacious interior; fourteenth-century effigy of William Harrington, and a Tyrwhitt brass of c. 1480. An inscription at the west end records the gift to the church of a clock, by Colonel Whichcote, as a thank-offering for the victory of Culloden (1746); the original clock was later removed to Aswarby (seat of the Whichcotes), and another clock presented in its place.

Harrington With its Tudor porch tower and long rows of eighteenth-century sash windows, Harrington Hall stands in its gardens of legendary beauty: there are raised terraced walks, and Tennyson associations ('Come into the garden, Maud'). The little church next door was almost entirely rebuilt by S. S. Teulon in 1854. But the monuments to the Copledikes are the thing – a brass to Margaret Copledike of c. 1480, and a succession of Elizabethan monuments to follow; the last Copledike monument is of 1658, after which the family faded out, and the Amcotts took over. An idyllic place.

Hatcliffe A very pretty valley leads from Ravendale to Hatcliffe, but

January landscape: Haugham

there are many 'bijou' residences in the little village; a thirteenth-century church, with rough ironstone tower, and Victorianised chancel of 1861 (by Rogers and Marsden).

Hatton Well-wooded country, and a remote little village. The small church with its apse and tiny spire, all in bright red brick, is by James Fowler (1870).

Haugh A long drive across bumpy fields leads to the fragment of an ancient house, now a farm, and to the tiny church of chalk and green-stone. The farmhouse is all that remains of the old seat of the Bolle family, and is in origin Tudor. The little church has a Decorated south doorway with ogee arch, a blocked north doorway of c. 1200, and a narrow Norman chancel arch, leading into the chancel with its two interesting Jacobean monuments to the Bolles. Ledger stones, an alabaster figure of St Leonard, the patron saint, and a nineteenth-century corona all combine to make this a memorable little building.

Haugham Sweeping Wold countryside, and a most engaging church which from a short distance appears to be Louth itself, inexplicably removed from its valley five miles farther on. Indeed it is a conscious imitation, built by the Revd G. A. Chaplin, the incumbent – but in brick and stucco and reduced in size. The architect was W. A. Nicholson, and this church has much in common with his other churches at Raithby and Biscathorpe. The interior is replete with period furnishings, and bright enamelled glass. The building is now in the care of the Redundant Churches Fund.

Hawerby A lovely spot in the Wolds: the Hall is late eighteenth century. The little church stands nearby and is chiefly thirteenth century, but is redundant, and now used as a studio.

Haxey A big village on a low hill in the Isle of Axholme: the long street of red houses climbs slowly to the imposing east end of the church – which with its pinnacled tower appears externally all Perpendicular. Inside there is a late Norman nave, and much Victorian decoration in the chancel, a spacious and handsome church. Wide views over the desolate flatlands all around: the mysterious medieval 'Hood Game' is played here every year on the Epiphany.

Haugham: an early nineteenth-century interior

Healing A leafy village, with many modern bungalows – and the well-wooded park of Edwardian Healing Manor. The church was much rebuilt in 1874, but the tower is ancient, with a decorative crocketed ogee-arched entrance of 1840. Recent parish hall attached to the south side.

Heapham In the unknown, unvisited country between Gainsborough and the Cliff. The church stands alone in the fields, with a late Saxon tower, and other early features – and some solitary, unsophisticated beauty.

Heckington Heckington Church is one of the glories of Lincolnshire. It is enormous, a complete church in the Decorated style, all built at the same time, and owing its magnificence to the wealthy Bardney Abbey, which appropriated the church in 1345. Walk round the exterior and absorb its many details: the grand curvilinear windows, the great crocketed pinnacles, the traceried parapets, the south porch with its carvings, the many buttresses everywhere, and finally the chancel with its east window of seven lights, comparable with those at Carlisle and Selby. The tremendous tower and spire dominate the landscape, already studded with noble spires. The interior has been somewhat spoilt by the Victorians: it is scraped, re-roofed, green and dim with indifferent glass, but its scale and spaciousness are overwhelming, and the Easter sepulchre, carved elaborately with the figures of the sleeping soldiers,

Heckington: the south porch and (right) Easter sepulchre

Helpringham (John Piper, Tate Archive)

the Marys, and Our Lord, is justly famous: opposite are sedilia and piscina of equal splendour.

Heckington is a large village of red brick; there is an eight-sailed windmill in working order.

Heighington There are one or two good houses in the village; the church is a curiosity – part medieval, part Victorian, part church, part school, so used as the result of an endowment left by Thomas Garrett, a fen drainage adventurer, 'for the teaching of Grammer and Latin in the Chapel of Heighington' in 1619.

Helpringham The wonderful spires of Asgarby, Heckington and Helpringham all greet each other across the level landscape. Helpringham is a beauty, with its flying buttresses, the base of the tower 'engaged' with the aisles. Most of the church is Decorated, with long clerestoried nave – but the interior is scraped, and spoiled by indifferent twentieth-century glass. However, there are seventeenth-century pews and pulpit to give pleasure.

Hemingby Over the little River Bain from Baumber – and there is Hemingby, very prettily set against a backcloth of trees: a little church, much rebuilt in 1764, and again in 1895, the early eighteenth-century almshouses founded by Jane Lady Dymoke, and a public house providing Bateman's Good Honest Ales.

Hemswell The village – with its maypole – is below the Cliff; not much of the medieval church survives. The tower is eighteenth century, and the rest appears externally Victorian. But inside, the nave arcade is thirteenth century, and there is a fourteenth-century sedilia.

Heydour A secluded valley, and a tiny hamlet: the large church with its lofty spire is Early English, Decorated and Perpendicular. There is important fourteenth-century glass, and a wealth of monuments to the Newtons of Culverthorpe in the north chapel. Two by Rysbrack, two by Scheemakers, they are to be discovered only by the persistent seeker, hidden behind the organ, approached through an old baize door.

The Old Vicarage is an extraordinarily attractive Victorian house by William White, and opposite is the early sixteenth-century priory house, with a carving of a cat and a salmon in the spandrels of the front door. Culverthorpe Hall – to the east – is an important and little known seventeenth-and eighteenth-century house standing in its park, overlooking a sheet of water. The steep-pitched roof of the central block gives the house a decidedly French look; the lower side wings, each with its Venetian window, appear English and Palladian. There are handsome interiors, with distinguished plasterwork. And at Oasby – to the west – is a small stone manor house of early Tudor date, with a shallow oriel window on the first floor.

Hibaldstow High marks to the parish for actually *building* a new tower – designed by Lawrence Bond – to the Victorian church in 1958-60; this in an age of little faith and little courage. The original tower fell in 1876, when the nave was rebuilt by James Fowler; the Early English tower arch survives, heavily restored. The village takes its name from St Hibald, Abbot of Bardney, who is buried here. During the rebuilding of the chancel in 1864 a large stone coffin was unearthed, containing the skeleton of a man 'of powerful frame' and a crozier. Who but St Hibald?

High Toynton Prominent by the roadside as the Skegness traffic passes: a Victorian greenstone church by Ewan Christian (1872), with a curious porch tower surmounted by a low octagonal spire.

Hogsthorpe A Marshland village, not far from the sea. The church is a

Heydour: monument to Sir Michael Newton by Scheemakers

patchwork of greenstone and old brick; much of the building is Early English, as is the lower part of the tower – the top stage is Perpendicular, as is the porch; Victorian chancel (1870). Inside, a Perpendicular font, and a Georgian pulpit.

Holbeach Another Fen church of great magnificence – of special interest for its architectural style: here Decorated can be seen clearly merging into Perpendicular. A lofty broach spire, set back behind a battlemented parapet, the north porch guarded by two intriguing low round towers. Inside, elegant tall nave arcades with clerestory of paired lights, great windows elsewhere with curvilinear tracery, and the fourteenth-century tomb of Sir Humphrey Littlebury.

The little town was the birthplace in 1687 of William Stukeley, antiquary and FRS, one of the Founders of the Society of Antiquaries.

Holbeach St Luke, Holbeach St Matthew and Holbeach St Mark Between Holbeach and the Wash are the little communities of St Luke, St Matthew and St Mark. Each is its own little charming world, each has its own small Victorian church of red brick – St Matthew and St Mark both by Ewan Christian (1897), St Mark's specially attractive with its apse and colourful Victorian glass, and a recent window to Canon C. V. Browne-Wilkinson, who from 1927 spent a lifetime here. From here it is possible to drive to the seabank, and climb up to survey the Wash – Hunstanton visible to the east, Boston Stump to the west.

Holton Beckering A worthwhile church, often dismissed as 'over-restored' (by Sir G. G. Scott). The south aisle is adorned outside with two pairs of heraldic shields, and there is much medieval work within. But the beauty of the church is undoubtedly Victorian – with delightful glass (by Clayton and Bell and others), excellent furnishings, and glorious reredos and sanctuary, glittering with mosaic and soft-coloured tiles.

Holton-le-Clay Suburban growth from Grimsby along the main road, and into the village; the church is an attractive patchwork of medieval stone and eighteenth-century brick, with an early tower and Norman font.

Holton-le-Moor 'The church is a small decayed building' wrote William White in his *Directory* (1842); the present elegant Early English and Decorated building is the work of G. G. Place (1854) and H. G. Gamble (1912), but it retains a Norman south doorway, and other medieval fragments.

Holton Beckering: reredos by Sir George Gilbert Scott

The Hall in its park is a late eighteenth-century brick house, and was the home of that distinguished Lincolnshire antiquary, George Dixon (d. 1970); unfortunately he never wrote a book, and all his learning remained in his head, or on scraps of paper or old envelopes – all of which, after his death, were reverently transported to the County Archives Office, and perhaps may one day be calendared.

Holywell The tiny church stands on the front lawn of the Hall, and is now the private property of the demesne. It is charming, built c. 1700 of remains of the medieval chapel of Aunby, and together with the temples and other little festive buildings serves as a wonderful garden ornament.

Honington A small village of stone cottages, stone walls and leafy lanes – and a Roman camp on the Heath above. The church is approached through the Old Vicarage garden: an Early English tower, with pinnacled Perpendicular top, a Norman nave, and a long narrow Early English chancel – full of interest on account of its Hussey monuments in the north-east chapel, and beautiful furnishings everywhere.

Horbling A spruce and attractive village on the edge of the Fens, and a noble cruciform church, with late Norman central tower. Inside, the crossing arches are a wonderful sight – wildly out of the perpendicular. Early English nave with Perpendicular clerestory, Decorated and Perpendicular transepts – in the north transept an elaborate fifteenth-century tomb, with sculpture of the Resurrection above; some good eighteenth-century monuments and hatchments.

Horkstow Sacred ground to lovers of horses and horse paintings, for here George Stubbs lived for several years in the 1750s, dissecting his horses, and making accurate drawings of the anatomy of the horse. Some of his best early paintings were done here, under the patronage of the Nelthorpes and Yarboroughs. The church has a pantiled tower, and climbs the western slope of the Wolds, so that the chancel is well above the level of the nave. Inside, Early English arcades and chancel arch; the chancel, though rebuilt externally in brick, is in origin Early English also, and is impressive with its steps leading up and up to the altar; Admiral Shirley's vault adds to the effect.

To the north Horkstow Hall is an imposing miniature-grand eighteenth-century house, close to the road, and former home of the Shirleys; there is lonely country to the west, where the suspension bridge (1844) crosses the New River Ancholme.

Horncastle Delightful little streets of unassuming Georgian houses lead from all directions into the Market Place; in the narrow High Street is a grand three-storeyed Georgian house, now shops, but once the town house of Sir Joseph Banks of Revesby.

Just off the Market Place is the church, all of greenstone, with an embattled tower (Early English and Decorated) capped with a little lead-covered spire. Outwardly the rest of the church appears all Perpendicular, extensively restored in the nineteenth century – but inside there are earlier arcades (Early English); a hefty Victorian chancel arch by Ewan Christian (1860) seems an intrusion, but sets the seal on his restoration. It is a spacious, towny interior, and there are monuments to see. In the north aisle is the brass to Sir Lionel Dymoke of Scrivelsby (1519), Champion of England; in the south aisle the unusual painted wooden tablet to Sir Ingram Hopton, the Royalist, slain at the Battle of Winceby in 1643: 'He paid his debt to nature and duty to his King and Country in the attempt of seizing the arch rebel in the bloody skirmish near Winceby, October 6th 1643.' In the chancel is another unusual monument, large and awe-inspiring, in white marble with heavy draperies of black, to George Heald (1834). And there are a number of hatchments, recently beautifully cleaned and restored.

Horsington The church appears an an extraordinary apparition across the flat lands near the River Witham – an expensive-looking towny building in bright red brick of 1860, with prominent broach spire, designed by David Brandon, who also built the rectory and school: an ambitious scheme for a scattered community.

Hough-on-the-Hill has a mighty Saxon tower, with one of the only four semi-circular extruding staircase turrets in all England (another is at Broughton in north Lincolnshire, the other two at Brixworth and Brigstock in Northamptonshire). Whitewashed atmospheric interior of distinguished Saxon proportions; there are old roofs throughout, and an enchanting inscription to a boy baronet, Sir Anthony Thorold, who died at eleven in 1721 'much lamented by all who know him, being a very promising child of wit and learning'. (See frontispiece.)

Hougham The church stands grand and solitary by the River Witham; a Saxon cross-shaft forms a lintel for the south doorway; a lofty spacious nave, with a perfect Norman arcade, leads to a Georgian chancel; there is a Crusader tomb, a rare Norman-Revival font dated 1662, and a number of later monuments to Thorold rectors. All was beautifully restored by Temple Moore early this century. The fragment of the

Hougham in the snow

medieval moated manor house of the Bussey and Brudenell families (with a Norman pillar in a sitting-room) has some Gothic tracery in a barn; enormous late Georgian Old Rectory, in its setting of ancient cedar trees.

Howell A tiny village – a farm or two, some cottages, and a diminutive medieval church, with bellcote, Norman south doorway, Transitional nave arcade, and Decorated chancel. The font is late Decorated, adorned with shields of arms; there are many early inscribed slabs, and the Jacobean tomb of Sir Charles Dymoke (d. 1602).

Humberston Caravans near the sea, and expensive villas elsewhere . . . The church is brick, of 1722, a fine big Georgian box, attached to a Perpendicular tower of stone. Inside is the grand monument to Matthew Humberston (d. 1709). The inscription tells us that he acquired an ample fortune in the Custom House 'with great honour and reputation', and left £1,000 for rebuilding the church. Too much poor modern furnishing and carpeting.

Humby, Great see **Great Humby**

Hundleby The long village street joins on to Spilsby; there are several attractive houses. The church was almost rebuilt in 1854; the base of the tower and the nave arcade survive from the medieval building.

Huttoft The church described by Sir John Betjeman in 'A Lincoln-shire Church'. Few words are needed to add to the late Laureate's description – except to mention the remarkable font, adorned with angels and figures of the twelve Apostles with hair like Struwwelpeter; the curious carved animals (?) which adorn the buttresses; and the eighteenth-century brick chancel. The interior is over-restored: gloomy, piney and tiled. The Indian Christian priest was the Revd Theophilus Caleb.

Hykeham, North see **North Hykeham**

Hykeham, South see **South Hykeham**

Immingham Everybody thinks of Immingham as a large and bustling port, and it is now hard to find the old village behind the enormous growth of docks, chemical works and oil refineries which line the Humber bank. Immingham Dock was the brainchild of the Great Central Railway – which decided to defy Hull across the water, and build a graving dock which would be the wonder of the world. The first dock was opened in 1913, the latest in 1960. Behind this new town it is possible to discover the ancient church; this has a pinnacled Perpendicular tower, but there is Norman work within, and the nave is thirteenth-century. Between the windows of the clerestory are eighteenth-century oil paintings of the Apostles.

Ingham A modest little church in a big village: Fillingham, Cammeringham, Ingham – there is something in the rhythm of these village names. There was once a much larger medieval church on this site, with a tower, but it fell on hard times, and was rebuilt in 1792, and then Gothicised and Victorianised in 1896. The result is a dull little building – but it is devout and devotional, and soaked in prayer.

Ingoldmells Butlin's Holiday Camp: this, a remarkable development of the '30s, and acres of caravans, crowd the coastline: the village is all dedicated to the summer holiday business. The church is a grand building of the thirteenth century, with nave arcades of six bays, and an early fourteenth-century tower with Perpendicular top. But, as at Addlethorpe, the chancel was pulled down in the early eighteenth century by the same lazy incumbent. Inside, a good Perpendicular font, old benchends, and a brass of 1520 to William Palmer with his crutch.

Ingoldsby The church with its solid tower has a certain massive attractiveness; there is Norman and Perpendicular work – and also some unusual rebuilding of the seventeenth century. A stone village in by-roads.

Irby-in-the-Marsh A small church with solid tower of greenstone – in origin medieval, but repaired in Georgian brick, with a chancel of 1886; altogether a delightfully textured ensemble.

Irby-on-Humber Just off the main road (A46) to Grimsby: the church clock chimes the quarters, and, inside, there are two twelfth-century arcades, a Norman font, and inscribed slabs.

Irnham A mysterious, exceptionally pretty estate village: the Hall, an important and little-known early sixteenth-century house, in turn the home of Thimelbys, Conquests, Arundells, and Cliffords, was a Roman Catholic house till its sale in 1858, and Mass was said in the attic throughout the penal times; two eighteenth-century Roman priests lie buried in the church. This is a grand building with Norman, Early English, Decorated and Perpendicular work; there are two medieval brasses, many later monuments, an exceptional Easter sepulchre, and a vivid Victorian east window of 1859. (See also Corby Glen.)

Keal, East see **East Keal**

Keal, West see **West Keal**

Keddington Bumpy fields beside the old Louth Canal; the little medieval church of stone patched with brick, which contains Norman and Early English work, has been much Victorianised – but there is a rare fifteenth-century wooden eagle lectern. In the churchyard, to the south-west of the church, is the grave of Jack Yates, with its delightful inscription. Prep school master, Member of the British Council, bon viveur, this much-loved figure gave the last years of his life to his native Louth, where he ran Goulding's Bookshop, and lived in the Mansion, the most beautiful house in Westgate. He was joint author of the *Shell Guide*, which is much quoted in these pages.

Keelby A large village, close to Brocklesby: the church is ancient, somewhat restored in the nineteenth century, with Perpendicular tower and early thirteenth-century south arcade; Elizabethan monuments to the South family, fragments of whose medieval house are incorporated in Church End Farm. Unattractive parish hall recently added to the south aisle of the church: it is difficult to conceive how such an addition could be made to a medieval church.

Kelby A diminutive stone village, close to the Ancaster stone quarries, and a little church which contains Norman and Decorated work, and has an embattled tower and recessed spire. What is unexpected is the Decorated south aisle with its vaulted roof. Many old poppyheads in the nave.

Kelsey, North see **North Kelsey**

Kelsey, South see **South Kelsey**

Kelstern Exhilarating Wold country: a handful of cottages, and the Hall – on its east side a Victorian rebuilding of what is clearly an Elizabethan house, on its west, facing the lane, a medley of older brick chimneys. The east front surveys a bumpy meadow, and the church on its low hillock. A Perpendicular tower – the rest somewhat over-restored in 1886. But it is beautifully furnished, and contains a good monument to Elizabeth South (1604) and three windows by Sir Ninian Comper to members of the Sleight family.

Kettlethorpe A romantic spot, embowered in ancient trees: Hall and church are at the end of the lane. The Hall is but a rebuilt fragment of an earlier house, reduced to a small hunting box in the nineteenth century – but in front stands the medieval gateway, the relic of the great medieval house of the Swynfords: Katherine Swynford was third wife of John of Gaunt. The church is a white brick box of 1809, attached to a medieval tower, with iron stanchions dividing nave from north aisle – but attractive in its way, with its late seventeenth-century French pulpit, some interesting monuments, and a beautiful carved corbel in the sanctuary, with an angel bearing the quartered shield of England and France.

Killingholme The church is at North Killingholme, the Humber bank not far away, alive with industry. A splendid tower, Norman at its base, Perpendicular at its top. Perpendicular nave arcades, Decorated traceried windows in the aisles, a pleasantly whitewashed interior.

Kingerby Remote and leafy. The Hall belonged for centuries to recusant families, so the parish church has remained untouched by nineteenth-century restorers. It seems wonderfully ancient, wonderfully textured, wonderfully detached from this present world. The tower is in origin Saxon, the nave Early English, the chancel Decorated; there are old roofs, old benchends, some fourteenth-century effigies, some fifteenth-century glass. It is now in the care of the Redundant Churches Fund.

Kirkby, East see **East Kirkby**

Kirkby Green A little stone church of 1848, simple and scholarly in design – the east end (according to Archdeacon Bonney) reproducing its medieval predecessor, with its lancet windows and vesica above. A devout interior, with west gallery.

Kirkby Laythorpe A modest, unassuming church with a low tower: this and the aisle windows are all Decorated, but there is a Norman south doorway, a Transitional nave arcade, a Victorian chancel, and some old benchends and other medieval woodwork.

Kirkby Underwood Well-wooded, gently undulating countryside – hence its name. The church stands by itself up a lane from the centre of the village, all spruce Early English and Perpendicular, with modest tower and seventeenth-century pulpit.

Kirkby-cum-Osgodby Unfrequented countryside. The parish church has an Early English tower and chancel, but the nave was rebuilt in 1825. In the chancel are two important tombs, one to John Wildbore who died in 1398: he lies in armour, his feet resting on a wild boar, and his wife under an ogee canopy, with angels by her pillow.

In 1793 the Youngs of Kingerby (*q.v.*) built a Roman Catholic chapel here – the earliest Catholic church in Lincolnshire. It takes the form of a large upper room in the wing of a red brick Georgian house. It is a beautiful interior, with a screen of Doric columns forming the sanctuary. A holy place.

Kirkby-on-Bain John Betjeman wrote 'A Lincolnshire Tale' after staying with the Blakistons at Kirkby-on-Bain (where the Revd F. M. Blakiston was incumbent). It begins

Kirkby with Muckby-cum-Sparrowby-cum-Spinx
Is down a long lane in the county of Lincs . . .

The village straggles in the watery meadows of the Bain: the small church – 'in a debased Gothic style' (Kelly) – was rebuilt in 1802; it is homely, built in greenstone, with Victorian bellcote, porch and chancel.

Kirkstead Across the bumpy fields, and past the gaunt fragment of the south transept of the ruined Abbey, stands St Leonard's Chapel, the *capella ante portas* of the great Cistercian house. It is an exquisite, tiny, vaulted Early English church, with narrow lancets, delicately carved capitals upon elegant dwarf shafts, wonderful and elaborate bosses.

Kirkstead: St Leonard's Chapel

Kirkstead: thirteenth-century vaulting and screen

Moreover, it is beautifully furnished, and the thirteenth-century screen is one of the earliest in England. A very precious little church.

Kirmington Brocklesby country: the church has an Early English tower with a very unexpected copper spire of 1838. Teulon restored the church in 1859, but inside there are some remarkable original capitals to the piers of the Decorated north arcade – heads and busts and other highly decorative grotesques.

Kirmond-le-Mire lies in a dip – a very muddy dip before it was drained: the main road goes up and down and up again to Binbrook; there are old farms, barns, and red brick walls – and a small church by W. A. Nicholson of 1847; but neither so inventive nor so playful as his earlier churches (*e.g.* Biscathorpe).

Kirton-in-Holland Once a market town, now caught up in Boston suburbia; but a few eighteenth-century (or earlier) houses survive in the wide street, ruined by the traffic of the A16. Prints survive of the magnificent cruciform medieval church in its original state, with grand Perpendicular central tower, nave, transepts, chancel. In 1804 the architect William Hayward performed on the church an almost incredible surgical operation. The central tower, considered dangerous (though in the end gunpowder was needed), was pulled down, the transepts destroyed, and the chancel shortened. Hayward then built the present Perpendicular west tower, so successfully that it easily passes for an ancient one. The interior is impressive and numinous, with a six-bay Early English nave with lofty circular piers. Beautiful furnishings, including west gallery of 1907: a solemn, devotional church.

Kirton-in-Lindsey A decayed little town, tumbling down the side of the Cliff: the church, with its grand and impressive Early English tower, stands below; there is a Norman priest's doorway, an Early English and Decorated nave, and Early English chancel; but there has been much Victorian restoration (by Ewan Christian and J. H. Hakewill, 1861).

Knaith Thomas Sutton, founder of the Charterhouse, was born here in 1532. The Hall is a long, low, ancient house, all done up in pretty Regency Gothic in the early nineteenth century, and the little church, fragment of a Cistercian nunnery, is on the lawn in front of the house, where the Trent flows by. It is a charming, odd little fragment, with a perfect Jacobean pulpit and other contemporary furnishings.

Kyme, North see **North Kyme**

Kyme, South see **South Kyme**

Laceby A large undistinguished village close to Grimsby: a church of many dates, much Victorianised. There is a five-bay Early English north arcade – the centre bay Norman: an odd man out. Archbishop Whitgift, a native of Grimsby, was once rector here.

Langrick The grandest of Jephtha Pacey's Fen chapels (1828): a nave with buttresses and Gothic windows traceried in white painted wood, a diminutive chancel, west porch and gabled bellcote – all in an attractive churchyard beside the main road, with trees and headstones.

Langtoft A large village on the edge of the Fens: Early English, Decorated and Perpendicular church, with clerestoried nave, and old plain glass and woodwork; the great west window displays a wonderful area

Langtoft: the Georgian porch

of evening sun-drenched glass. Brass candelabra, and good seven-teenth/eighteenth-century monuments. The spire is curiously set at the west end of the north aisle, and the south porch is an attractive early eighteenth century addition.

Langton-by-Horncastle A little church of greenstone, with blocked up north arcade, a medieval font made up of fragments from Kirkstead Abbey, and handsome Victorian pulpit and lectern carved by a former incumbent: a delightful spot.

Langton-by-Partney The squire's church, and one of the most perfect eighteenth-century churches anywhere. Built c. 1700 of warm red brick, with wide overhanging eaves, and a low octagonal bell tower at the west end (an odd later alteration), the interior is arranged like a college chapel, with box pews, a three-decker pulpit, curved Communion rails, and reredos with fluted Corinthian pilasters: the woodwork is of superb quality. The Langtons of Langton have been here since the reign of Henry II; their Tudor house was burnt down in the early nineteenth century, and the Victorian house which took its place was pulled down after the Second World War. The present squire lives in the white house guarded by the thatched *cottage ornée* lodge near the church. In the eighteenth century Bennet Langton was a close friend of Dr Johnson, who often stayed here: it is a pleasure to think of the learned doctor worshipping here in the squire's church.

Langton-by-Wragby A Perpendicular tower, and a small church rebuilt by Atkinson in 1866, to replace an eighteenth-century building. Two attractive seventeenth-century monuments within.

Langworth An untidy growth along the main road from Lincoln to Wragby. The only building of note is the exceptionally interesting church – a rebuilding by Haynes and Johnson of Brigg (1960-2) of the chapel at Walmsgate Hall near Louth, built in 1901 by Mr Dallas-Yorke in memory of his son Francis, killed in the South African War. The architect of this was Henry Wilson: his are the magnificent doors with their bronze handles, the hanging lamps, the organ, the font, the marble floor, the high altar with its baldacchino, and the memorial to the young officer forming the west gallery. It is a little building of the greatest charm: the Art Nouveau decoration is exquisite.

Art Nouveau at Langworth

Bodley at Laughton

Laughton Remote, secluded, well-wooded countryside close to the Trent. A remarkable church, one of three 'Meynell' churches, founded, or in this case refounded, by the Hon. Mrs Meynell-Ingram of Hoar Cross (Staffordshire). All are the work of Bodley. Here, in 1896, he found a dilapidated medieval church: to the Perpendicular tower and original medieval arcades he added a clerestory and new roof, and splendid lofty chancel, in his own characteristic Decorated or Perpendicular style. Rood screen, gorgeous towering reredos, organ case, are all Bodley's, as are also the beautiful sanctuary furnishings. Recumbent effigy of Hugo Francis Meynell-Ingram – a replica of the one at Hoar Cross – by Thomas Woolner; fifteenth-century brass, and sixteenth-century Dalison tomb. A very special church, not to be missed.

Lea Now caught up in the suburbia of Gainsborough, but the village itself is still pretty. The Hall, home for many generations of the Andersons, baronets extinct, a Victorianised Elizabethan brick house, has been pulled down. The church has a Perpendicular tower, but was much restored by Pearson. It is chiefly Early English and Decorated. There is a little medieval glass in the north aisle, and an array of monuments to the Andersons, with interesting inscriptions.

Leadenham From the west, Leadenham House and Leadenham Church

Leadenham: the Perpendicular spire

form a splendid group on the shelf of the Cliff, with the well-wooded hillside rising behind; especially so on a summer evening, lit up by the setting sun. The church has a noble Perpendicular spire; the rest is handsome Decorated work. Of special interest is the chancel ceiling, painted by Pugin with his own hand in 1841; the early sixteenth-century glass in the upper lights of the east window was brought from Belgium in 1834 (the rest of the window is by Hardman, and also good). There are seventeenth-century monuments to the Beresfords, and later ones to the Reeves of Leadenham House, a distinguished military family.

Leake, Old see **Old Leake**

Leasingham A large village, ruined by traffic and bungalows, but a church with a noble Early English tower surmounted by a magnificent broach spire. Interior scraped and Victorianised; there is a bust of Bishop Trollope, Bishop Suffragan of Nottingham (when, for a brief period, Nottinghamshire was included in the Lincoln Diocese), local antiquary, and builder of the almshouses. There are several good houses in the village.

Legbourne On the edge of the Marsh, a suburbanised village. But the Decorated church is handsome, though much restored by Rogers and Marsden (1868). Perpendicular font, Perpendicular screen, fragments of medieval glass.

Legsby The lower slopes of the Wolds. The church stands alone at the edge of a field, with its odd little pinnacled tower, and curious Georgian proportions; in fact it is in origin medieval, but much rebuilt in the early nineteenth century.

Lenton Lonely village on the uplands south-east of Grantham; the church stands well, with its Decorated broach spire. The nave is Early English, and in the chancel is the remarkable tomb to the Armyne family of Osgodby: a most unusual piece of Tudor Renaissance design (1605), it rises like a great reredos, adorned with little Corinthian columns, many shields of arms, and long inscriptions.

Leverton One of the distinguished churches between Boston and Wainfleet – outwardly all Perpendicular with its west tower, clerestoried nave, elaborate chancel and south chapel. Inside, however, the arcades are Decorated. The chancel is the glory of the church, with its lavishly carved and vaulted sedilia, and adjoining chantry chapel, Perpendicular font and screen – a wide interior, now somewhat overcarpeted.

Leverton: sedilia

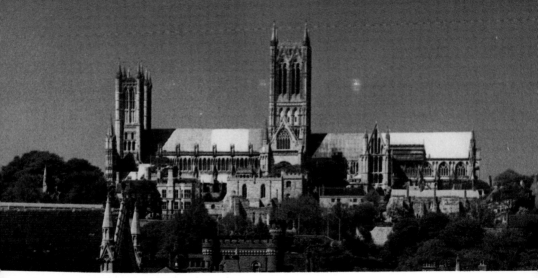

Lincoln on its hill

Lincoln on its hill: it is amazing how the Cathedral accompanies the traveller all day as he drives around the county. Approaching Lincoln from the south, along the lonely Brant road, the sight of the Cathedral ahead across the cornfields is reminiscent of the distant view of Chartres across the wide cornfields of central France. If he makes his way north towards Gainsborough, the Cathedral still dominates the view – not the long south front now, but the west front, peering over the brow of the hill. If he turns his steps east, and makes for Caenby Corner, the Cathedral will still be following him round: here it will again be the three towers, but this time the full length of the north side – and, on climbing the Wolds near Tealby, on a clear day the distant view of the Cathedral will still be with him, and as he makes his way south along the brow of the Wolds, the Cathedral will still be there, in sharp outline, which will become nearer and nearer, and clearer and clearer as he travels south. On a clear day the Cathedral is visible over half the county.

   This is a book about the parish churches of Lincolnshire – but a few words must be said about the Cathedral. Lincoln Cathedral is a giant: standing in the Bail, the square outside the Castle, the west towers rise above the Exchequer Gate. They are Norman below, fourteenth century above, rising above the thirteenth-century screen which, with its tier upon tier of blank arcading, envelops the original Norman west front, so clearly visible below with its round arches and remarkable sculpture. The visitor will stand before this stupendous west front, then walk round the exterior, examining towers, pinnacles, transepts, flying buttresses. Everything around is dominated by the building's gigantic

OPPOSITE *Lord Tennyson surveys Minster Yard under the shadow of the Cathedral*

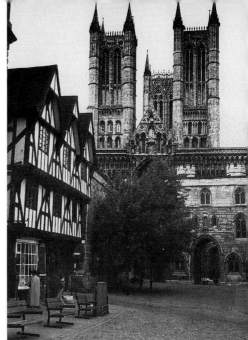

The Bishop's Eye and (right) The Bail and Exchequer Gate, Lincoln

presence. Inside, awestruck, he will gaze at the arcades, traceried windows, medieval woodwork, the vast spaces. The nave belongs to the first half of the thirteenth century: the bays are wide, typically English – and the triforium has broad low openings, the vaulting a complex palmlike pattern of ribs. The Great Transept is perhaps the most impressive part of the whole Cathedral – large enough to contain nave and chancel of some lesser cathedral. At either end is a vast rose window – the Bishop's Eye, the Dean's Eye – filled with magical medieval glass. Below the former is Sir William Richmond's splendid bronze figure of the saintly Bishop King (d. 1910).

The original central tower collapsed in 1237; the two lower stages were rebuilt soon after; the upper stage was built in 1307, and was originally crowned with a lead spire (as were the western towers). The spire on the central tower collapsed in 1548, the western spires were removed in 1807 – but they appear in old prints. Standing under the central tower, the narrow doorway in the pulpitum leads into St Hugh's Choir, built at the very end of the twelfth century, with its curious, early, lop-sided vaulting, its double arcading in the aisles, and, of course, the choir stalls – one of the two or three finest sets of medieval stalls in England (c. 1350). Beyond is the Angel Choir (consecrated in 1280) – one of the greatest monuments of English Geometrical work, and built to house St Hugh's Shrine. The high altar reredos is by James Essex

(1769), and the glass in the east window by Ward and Hughes (1855). All around are chapels (in the narrow eastern transepts) and chantries; one of these, St Blaise Chapel, was decorated with murals by Duncan Grant in 1958. The north-east transept leads to the cloisters and chapter house – the earliest of the English octagonal chapter houses (early thirteenth century) – and octagonal chapter houses were a purely English invention. The north side of the cloisters is occupied by the Wren Library (1674), standing on an almost Italianate loggia; bay trees grown in tubs adorn the colonnade below. 'I have always held' wrote Ruskin 'and am prepared against all comers to maintain, that the Cathedral of Lincoln is out and out the most precious piece of architecture in the British Isles, and roughly speaking worth any two other cathedrals we have.'

Lincoln is two cities – above hill, and below. From above, the view is of factories and chimneys and rows of drab streets. Lincoln grew enormously in the nineteenth century. But from the lower town there are views of the Cathedral sailing above – among the greatest sights in Europe. At the top of the High Street in the lower town the medieval Stonbow leads up to Steep Hill, a perilous ascent to the upper town: beyond Bailgate the Newport Arch guards the northern entrance, the Roman gate to the Roman city of Lindum Colonia.

Three ancient churches line the High Street in the lower town – each with a Saxon tower: St Benedict, a beautiful Early English fragment; St Mary-le-Wigford, Early English and Decorated, close to the railway station; and St Peter-at-Gowts, farther south, a very early church, Norman and Early English. Still farther south, St Botolph's has an eighteenth-century tower, but the church is a remodelling by William Watkins (1870).

Of later churches, St Mary Magdalene, close to the Exchequer Gate, is in origin medieval, but much rebuilt by Bodley in 1882; St Nicholas, near the Newport Arch, is by Sir Gilbert Scott (1838) – one of his earliest churches; and St Michael's, off Steep Hill, is by S. S. Teulon (1853) at his most restrained; St Peter-in-the-Eastgate is by Sir A. W. Blomfield (1870), with a beautiful south aisle by Temple Moore (1914); St Faith's is by Hodgson Fowler (1895) – a good church in a drab district; and All Saints', also by Hodgson Fowler, is an imposing, lofty church (1904), with later furnishings by Comper – a lovely church. St Swithin's, so conspicuous with its lofty spire, is a very large church by James Fowler (1870); St Giles's is a rebuilding of St Peter-at-Arches (by Smith of Warwick, 1724) in a new housing estate, 1936.

Boultham is a submerged village: the old village church is small, in origin medieval, but the chancel was rebuilt in 1864, and the rest much restored by Hodgson Fowler in 1887. Holy Cross is the new and much larger parish church (1940 by Lawrence Bond), a pleasant 1930s Gothic building.

Bracebridge is another: here the church has a Saxon tower, and a narrow Saxon chancel arch – the rest is Early English; well restored by Pearson in 1875.

Linwood A church with a spire – rare in these parts – and dedicated to St Cornelius, also a rarity. Tower and spire are Perpendicular, nave Early English, and chancel Victorian. Of special note are two brasses (1419 and 1421) to John Lyndewode and his wife, and to another John Lyndewode – both of exceptional quality.

Lissington The church is at the corner, as the main road (B1202) turns right: a long low Georgian building (1796), of stone with brick dressings, and a small bellcote; an unsophisticated, very personal interior.

Little Bytham With its Norman tower and Perpendicular spire, and stonebuilt village grouped around, Little Bytham is a good sight from the high railway viaduct as the trains roar past on their way from King's Cross to Grantham and the North. Much Norman work in the church; priest's doorway with carved tympanum; Early English nave; sixteenth-century pulpit; old benchends. The church has the rare dedication to St Medard, sixth-century Bishop of Noyon in France.

Little Carlton 'The charm of 1837' wrote Jack Yates in the *Shell Guide* (1965): a small church with modest tower and spire, cemented. Abandoned, and now threatened with demolition. Feeble.

Little Cawthorpe Dramatically placed above the village with its 'splash' stands R. J. Withers's little church of 1860, all in red brick with bands of black, with a bell turret with spirelet and slate roof – inappropriate perhaps to its rural setting, but a building of considerable self-confident Victorian charm.

Little Coates Now in the Borough of Grimsby, and surrounded by suburban roads – but the church is one of considerable beauty and interest. To the ancient village church Sir Walter Tapper added, in 1914, a new nave with west tower, and an exceptionally beautiful vaulted chancel – rib-vaulted in the manner of the thirteenth century. A delightfully furnished interior with stalls and organ loft, the old church (chiefly Perpendicular) becoming the Lady Chapel. It is only a pity that the chancel vault has been insensitively painted blue.

Little Grimsby Like a little whitewashed shrine in Greece the tiny church stands sparkling amid trees in the garden of the Hall; above the west door is a datestone 1500, in eighteenth-century lettering. There is just a little nave, and a miniature chancel, with old roof, Nelthorpe and Beauclerk monuments and hatchments, pretty objects of piety, and one notable stained glass window, to Tom Wintringham, MP, who died in the House of Commons in 1921. Outside the door an urn, like a garden ornament, commemorates John Nelthorpe (1784). The Hall is a distinguished brick house of c. 1700, built by the Nelthorpes.

Little Ponton Wonderfully detached in its valley, watered by the little River Witham, for all the proximity of the Great North Road, and the main railway line. An odd little church, with no tower or bellcote, but a single bell in an alcove high in the west wall, dated 1657. Inside it is scraped and electrified, but otherwise Norman or Transitional. Monument in sanctuary to William Thorold (1725), a well-known recusant, who harboured Roman priests in the Hall: he is buried under the high altar. How many realise that a pious Papist squire lies here?

Little Steeping A pretty church, and a pretty spot – where the Marsh merges with the Fen. It is of greenstone and old brick, with a Perpendicular tower, the body of the church all Decorated and Perpendicular, the interior full of atmosphere, with its painted rood screen, painted roofs, and effigy of Thomas de Reding, a fourteenth-century rector, discovered in 1912, upside down, in use as the chancel step.

Londonthorpe In a splendid position, overlooking Belton Park. The church has one of the very few saddleback towers in Lincolnshire – a Victorian addition, and delightful. Much of the church is Early English or Decorated, but the clerestory is Perpendicular. A spruce Belton Estate village.

Long Bennington Nearly ruined by bungalows and other recent housing – but not so long ago a delightful village. Even now, bordering the long narrow greens on either side of the Old North Road, there are plenty of good-looking houses and cottages. The village is now by-passed.

The church is at the far south end – a handsome building. The nave arcades are late Norman, but the clerestory, porch and chancel are Perpendicular, as is the upper part of the bold pinnacled tower.

Long Sutton An attractive little town with wide Market Place, many eighteenth-century houses and early nineteenth-century terraces. The

Long Sutton: the highest, oldest, and most perfect lead spire in England.

church is one of the marvels of Lincolnshire, its lead spire justly cele-brated – 'the highest, oldest, and most perfect lead spire' in England, according to Dr J. Charles Cox. It crowns an early thirteenth-century detached tower, which originally had open arches. The noble nave consists of seven Norman bays with triforium and clerestory, but much of what surrounds it is Perpendicular. There is a curious two-storey sacristy at the north-east angle of the chancel. The early eighteenth-century reredos is banished to the north aisle, but the Communion rails survive *in situ*. Fragments of medieval glass; many eighteenth-century monuments.

Louth Of all the pleasures of Lincolnshire, a visit to Louth is one of the greatest: not only is it the perfect small market town – it possesses a church with one of the most glorious of all English spires, and to approach the place from any direction is an excitement not to be forgot-ten. Approach from Wragby: there is a point on the road (A156) where the Wolds unfold to reveal the spire rising from the gap. Or approach from Horncastle: turning the corner at the last lap before descending Breakneck Lane, the spire, close at hand, appears in all its power and glory, like a sudden apparition, dwarfing houses and trees and streets. Or come from the Marsh: the lonely twisting roads point to Louth, and it never seems to get any nearer – but there is the spire in the distance, pointing like a finger, pointing to Heaven, beckoning us on.

Almost any street in Louth is a pleasure, lined with Georgian or early Victorian houses or cottages, and every street leads to Mercer Row, and the Market Place, and the church. Come by Westgate, the best of them all, past a whole procession of grand houses: all the time the spire is confronting us with ever-increasing magnificence. It rises up, stage after stage of almost impossible beauty, to the enormous pinnacles which support the spire itself with flying buttresses, made, it would seem, of lace.

The spire is the latest of all the great medieval spires of England – 200 years after Grantham. It was begun in 1501, and completed in 1515; it cost £305.7s.5d. Inside, it is a thrill to stand under the tower, which with its great windows rises like a lantern; the church itself is a little earlier in date, and though wide and spacious (like the churches of the Marsh) is in some ways a little disappointing. An early nineteenth-century engraving shows the church filled with eighteenth-century Baroque furnishings; all looked well. James Fowler did away with all this, and replaced it with his own meagre Gothic fittings. A disaster. There is a memorial to him in the south chapel, with his head in profile, 'three times Mayor of Louth'.

Of the other churches, St Michael's is by him (1863), and is Fowler at his most ornate best. Holy Trinity is by Rogers and Marsden (1886), an imposing and rather bleak affair in rock-faced stone. The Roman Catholic church is a pretty little Gothic building of 1833, with presbytery attached.

Low Toynton A small abandoned church, all overgrown with ivy, its windows broken, its roof caving in – sad and shocking, but 'picturesque' and romantic; a few ancient features may yet be discerned.

Ludborough A fine big church, a prominent landmark on the main road from Louth to Grimsby – with a bold Perpendicular tower, and the body of the church Early English: beautiful long narrow lancets in the chancel. James Fowler restored the building in 1858 – for once a light-handed restoration.

Luddington The tall broach spire is a landmark across the desolate flatness of the Axholme landscape: a big church of 1855 in the fields, a long way from the village, detached, silent and enigmatic. One good eighteenth-century monument; colourful glass by Gibbs.

Ludford James Fowler again: a large church with transepts and bellcote astride the Louth-Gainsborough road; the somewhat chilly Victorian interior, and the south porch, are enlivened with highly decorative leaf carving.

Lusby An endearing little church, whose modest bellcoted exterior belies an interior of great archaeological interest – with Norman features and Saxon fragments, a Perpendicular screen, and a brass of 1555 with rhyming inscription.

Lutton A brick Perpendicular church – unusual for Lincolnshire – with tall tower and stone spire: an attractive composition. Dr Busby, Head Master of Westminster, was born here in 1606; the pulpit was his bequest (1702).

Mablethorpe 'A commodious bathing place on the coast of the German Ocean,' wrote William White in his *Directory* (1843), 'where the sands are smooth and firm.' The Tennyson family would come over from Somersby to enjoy the sands and the sea: it is hard to imagine them doing so now. During the late nineteenth century the place grew up into a 'kind of shack town', and is now a paradise for those from the northern towns who are in search of chalets, bathing huts and amusement booths, and the rows and rows of red houses stretch into the

OPPOSITE *Westgate, Louth*

countryside behind. Here stands the ancient village church – a remarkable sight with its high-pitched chancel roof higher than the squat tower: it is a medieval building, much patched with brick in the seventeenth century. There is a good tomb to Thomas Fitzwilliam (1494), and a brass to Elizabeth Fitzwilliam (1522).

Maltby-le-Marsh An interesting church of Marshland atmosphere: wide, unaisled early fourteenth-century nave, an abbreviated chancel, and Perpendicular tower. There is an early fourteenth-century effigy of a knight, and a remarkable Perpendicular font, bristling with angels and other figures.

Manby The village is concealed by the extensive buildings of the RAF Flying College (now closed – and used as council offices). The church is chiefly Perpendicular, with tall tower; chancel by Sir A. Blomfield (1889). Inside, a notable Anglo-Saxon slab, adorned with interlacing pattern, and a seventeenth-century font.

Manthorpe Almost overtaken by Grantham, but a charming little estate village, of pretty mid-nineteenth-century cottages, set against the plantations of Belton Park. Handsome stone church of 1848 by G. G. Place, with central spire.

Manton From the hillside there are distant views of the chimneys and furnaces of Scunthorpe. The little church of 1861 is by Hooker and Wheeler in elegant Decorated style – at its feet a warren of new houses and bungalows.

Mareham-le-Fen On the edge of the Fen – the most newly drained Fen close to Revesby. A large, spreading village, with a much restored church. However, there is a good deal to see: Early English tower with Perpendicular top, and highly decorative pinnacled exterior – also Perpendicular. Spacious interior, with fourteenth-century nave and chancel, somewhat Victorianised.

Mareham-on-the-Hill An unrestored church, indeed a forgotten church, of uncertain date, medieval in origin, done up in 1804 and fitted with box pews, two-decker pulpit, and so on, all at the end of a footpath, and through a farmyard.

Markby The only thatched church in Lincolnshire, tiny, medieval in origin, but much patched over the centuries – with seventeenth-century windows, and fragments re-used from Markby Priory, an Augustinian house founded in the twelfth century. Delightful interior with box pews, two-decker pulpit, and three-sided Georgian altar rails.

Markby, the only thatched church in Lincolnshire. BELOW *The interior.*

Market Deeping A delightful little town on the very frontier of North-amptonshire, with two wide streets of stone houses meeting at the crossroads, and the River Welland dividing the counties. The church has a Perpendicular tower, and is externally all Perpendicular; but inside there are earlier nave arcades, and unmistakable signs of James Fowler's restoration of 1875.

Market Rasen The church stands to the north of the Market Place, and has a Perpendicular tower, but the remainder of the building is externally all Victorian, the result of the restoration of 1862. A few ancient features survive, such as the Norman south doorway; inside it is the same story: the arcades are Perpendicular, but otherwise it is a Victorian church.

The town itself has its own quiet charm, but its houses are modest: only the Centenary Chapel of 1863, with its grand portico looking up Union Street, is in any way memorable.

Market Stainton A most endearing little medieval church of greenstone patched with brick; inside, a simple early nineteenth-century plaster ceiling to the nave, and an enchanting tiny plaster-vaulted chancel, complete with beautiful early twentieth-century glass and furnishings. A few modest monuments, and a tall early nineteenth-century font, the shape of a Victorian pillar box.

Marsh Chapel A grand Perpendicular church with bold west tower, and typical wide Marshland interior: that rare thing, a church built as one piece. The prosperity of these parts in the Middle Ages was due to the salt workings.

Marston Red-brick cottages by the River Witham. The church has a lofty thirteenth-century broach spire, medieval nave, and ornate Victorian chancel by Charles Kirk, who restored the church in 1880; there is handsome Victorian furnishing, glass by Ward and Hughes (1880), and one window by Christopher Whall (1897). There are Elizabethan tombs and later monuments to the Thorolds, who have held the manor since the fourteenth century. The Hall is their ancient home, though the chief seat of the baronet was transferred to Syston in the eighteenth century: Marston was reduced in size, and the Tudor Great Hall filled in with Georgian rooms. It is the home of the author of this book, and is surrounded by a romantic garden, with high hedges, unexpected vistas and old trees.

Martin A wide village street of white brick on the edge of the narrow

Marston: the thirteenth-century broach spire

Fen, and a bleak straight road across it to Woodhall Spa. The church was built in 1876 (tower 1911) by T. H. Wyatt, rock-faced, defiantly Victorian. A street of suburban houses opposite is called Wyatt Close; whoever thought of honouring the last of that distinguished architectural dynasty thus?

Martin by Horncastle Lost among the farm buildings, and all but concealed from view, a tiny, somewhat tattered little building of stone and brick, with a Norman doorway and a remarkable narrow chancel arch, Norman and Early English, opening into a dim-lit sanctuary. A precious, forgotten little building.

Marton A thrilling church: the severe Saxon tower stands like a sentinel over the main road from Lincoln to Gainsborough, rich in texture

Martin by Horncastle: the sanctuary

Saxon herringbone at Marton

with herringbone coursing. The interior is simple and solemn, with a narrow late Saxon (or early Norman) chancel arch, a later Norman north arcade, Early English south arcade, and a precious twelfth-century sculpture of the Crucifixion in the north wall of the sanctuary. There is a Perpendicular south porch, and Perpendicular embattlements and pinnacles adorn the exterior.

Mavis Enderby 'The Brides of Mavis Enderby' – Jean Ingelow's line from *The High Tide on the Coast of Lincolnshire* comes to mind: a delightful thought, and a delightful spot in the Wolds. The church is of greenstone, and with the curious dormer windows inserted by Fowler at his restoration (1875) appears largely Victorian outside. But much of the Perpendicular period survives within – a particularly attractive interior, beautifully furnished – with elaborate rood screen (with rood), and glorious angels to support the roof.

Melton Ross Beautiful rolling countryside. The church stands above the main road (A18), surrounded by evergreens, a small building by Ewan Christian (1867) with apse and bellcote; vintage dark Victorian interior.

Messingham A large dormitory village close to Scunthorpe: Victorian villas, and modern bungalows. The medieval church was largely rebuilt in 1818 (at his own expense) by the 'robber archdeacon', Dr Bayley, who was then rector and archdeacon of Stow; he 'plundered' neighbouring churches, and even more distant ones like Malvern Priory and Manchester Cathedral, to glorify his own. Hence the interesting medieval glass, and other furnishings.

Metheringham A large village. The great interest of the church is that it was rebuilt after a fire in 1601, and the nave arcades have Tuscan columns. Much Victorian restoration. Handsome monument to Sir Thomas Skipwith, 1763.

Middle Rasen A main road village, the church up a side street to the north. There is a prominent Perpendicular tower, and much of the building is Perpendicular, but the south doorway and chancel arch are Norman, and the north arcade Early English. Perpendicular rood screen, and fourteenth-century effigy of a priest holding a chalice.

Midville One of Jephtha Pacey's Fen chapels, with a small Georgian cupola, Gothic side windows, and the date 1819 firmly placed in the middle of its pedimented front.

Miningsby Pretty country, where the Wolds slope down to the Fens.

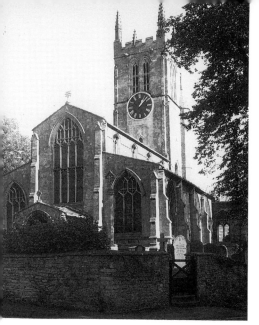

Morton (by Bourne) and (right) 'The Stoning of Stephen' by Burne-Jones at Morton (by Gainsborough)

But the little church which James Fowler restored in 1878 has been demolished, and the churchyard, full of graves, is empty and depressing.

Minting A secluded village, with an inn called The Sebastopol and a charming small church largely rebuilt by Ewan Christian in 1863. Inside, the Early English arcade survives, and an important cross-shaft of c. 1200, carved with the Crucifixion.

Moorby The little brick and stone church by Fowler (1866) has recently been demolished. Progress. It was an attractive building, and is sadly missed.

Morton *(by Bourne)* A stately cruciform church on the edge of the Fens, with a grand Perpendicular central tower, and an imposing west front surveying the length of the village street. Inside, lofty Early English and Decorated arcades in the clerestoried nave, and, beyond the fan-vaulted crossing, a long Decorated chancel. A great array of Victorian glass (by Powell and others) makes this majestic interior dark and mysterious.

Morton *(by Gainsborough)* The street leads down to the Trent: the church by Micklethwaite and Somers Clarke (1891) is attached to the tower surviving from the earlier church by T. Johnson (1841), and outwardly is unexciting. But inside it is a spacious and original building, worthy of its distinguished architects, and of Sir Hickman Bacon, the mind behind the rebuilding (see Gainsborough). Low arcades and a charmingly decorated plaster ceiling lead the eye to rood screen and high altar. All around is the sumptuous collection of windows by Burne-Jones and Morris. There are thirteen of them, of which perhaps the finest is that in the north transept depicting the stoning of Stephen. But all the furnishings are of merit: altars, organ case, font of Frosterley marble; a modest tablet in the south aisle commemorates Morton's great benefactor, Sir Hickman Bacon. Until his death in 1944 he attended the church each Sunday, and placed a gold sovereign in the plate – duly collecting it from the vestry after the service. At the end of the year he sent to the vicar a cheque for £52.

Moulton The village with its green, its old trees and a number of good houses, is an oasis in the flat, featureless Fens. The church has a magnificent crocketed Perpendicular spire with flying buttresses, and long nave with twelfth-century arcades and Early English clerestory. Baroque font (early eighteenth century), modelled on a design by Grinling Gibbons.

Moulton Chapel An octagonal chapel in the centre of this remote Fenland village, built in 1722 by William Sands of Spalding, for Maurice Johnson of Ayscoughee Hall. Victorian chancel, 1886.

Muckton A village 'twixt the Wolds and the Marsh. The church in the Norman Revival style of 1878 (by James Fowler) has been shamelessly destroyed. It possessed an imposing (genuine) Norman chancel arch.

Mumby Marshland. The church is Early English and of greenstone; the tower is Perpendicular, more distinguished and of ashlar; the chancel is Victorian. The interior is dominated by the rood screen (fifteenth century), with its loft and rood.

Navenby The church stands on the very edge of the Cliff. The tower collapsed c. 1750 – no wonder – and the present tower is an eighteenth-century replacement, a poor thing. But the rest of the church is magnificent: a Decorated nave with a Perpendicular clerestory, and a grand, spacious Decorated chancel, comparable with Heckington and Hawton (Notts): enormous traceried east window, and sedilia and Easter sepulchre gloriously adorned with exquisite carving. The Roman soldiers stand below, much mutilated, above, the Marys, worshipping angels, and, at the top, the figure of Our Lord. There is an elaborate font by Charles Kirk (1862), and a rood screen by Temple Moore (1910).

Navenby is a large and attractive village, with a wide street of stone houses with red pantiled roofs.

Navenby: Easter sepulchre

Nettleham A dormitory village for Lincoln: much new housing. The church is architecturally distinguished, especially the nave with its beautiful Early English arcades; the chancel was partly rebuilt by Bodley in 1882, and there was much handsome furnishing and decoration by him. Recent 're-ordering' – dreaded word – has spoiled the atmosphere of this delightful church. But there is good glass by Kempe.

On the far side of the main road stand the burnt-out fragments of the Hall, a Georgian house destroyed in a fire of 1937; and, now almost smothered in the undergrowth, the grand eighteenth-century gates from St Peter-at-Arches in Lincoln, removed here when that church was pulled down.

Nettleton A large village nestling under the Wolds where the A46 climbs up to Caistor. The church has a Saxon tower of ironstone, but the rest is a rebuilding by Fowler (1874), spacious and exuberant.

New Bolingbroke There is a fascination about the long straight roads that cross the most lately drained Fen here – drained in the early nineteenth century by Sir Joseph Banks (of Revesby) and John Rennie. New Bolingbroke is an odd little place founded in 1824 by John Parkinson, Sir Joseph's steward; there is a small crescent, and rows of cottages line the main road. The church is much later (1854), by S. S. Teulon, and characteristic of the man, with its violent red brick and sombre stone, and its little spire in the north-east corner. The Gothic vicarage behind the church is also his.

New York There is a signpost near Coningsby which proclaims BOSTON and NEW YORK; New York, Bunker's Hill – such are the names of two tiny Fen settlements. There is a little brick chapel of 1816, one of the first of these Fen chapels after the drainage – extremely simple, with pedimented west end, Gothic windows, and no bellcote; almost certainly the work of Jephtha Pacey.

Newton In forgotten, leafy countryside – a very pretty village: church, school, stone cottages stand informally round the green. At the far end, the Red Lion serves excellent food, and provides squash courts for those so inclined. The church has a tall tower (Early English and Perpendicular), and a dark, mysterious interior, medieval, with some Victorian restoration.

Newton-by-Toft A mile away from Toft-next-Newton (of course): a delightful pair. Newton-by-Toft is an endearing little church, tactfully restored by James Fowler in 1860; an intimate nave, a narrow Norman chancel arch, and a tiny chancel, bright with Victorian glass. Two miniature stone effigies (late thirteenth century).

Newton-on-Trent Dunham Toll Bridge across the river connects Nottinghamshire and Lincolnshire, Dunham on the west side, Newton on the east: it is like crossing a frontier between two countries. Newton Church has been much altered and rebuilt: 'a neat structure,' writes William White (1842), 'which has undergone some extensive repairs.' Exactly.

Nocton A sumptuous Victorian church, whose spire stands out prominently against the plantations of the Hall. It was built by Sir George Gilbert Scott in 1862 for the Countess of Ripon, in memory of her husband, the 1st Earl. The spire is 130 feet high, and the vaulted porch leads into a short nave, spacious and stately. The chancel is more wondrous, with marble shafts and elaborate capitals, the sanctuary aglow with mosaic and alabaster. There are magnificent candlesticks,

Nocton: Victorian splendour. BELOW *Sir George Gilbert Scott's reredos.*

grand pulpit and font, and excellent glass by Clayton and Bell. Moreover, there are interesting monuments: Sir William Ellys by William Stanton (1680); the 4th Earl of Buckinghamshire (1816), and his brother, the Dean of Windsor (1846). Finally there is the recumbent effigy, by Scott and Matthew Noble, of the 1st Earl of Ripon (1859), who as Viscount Goderich had been Prime Minister 1827-28.

'Nocton, a beautiful seat,' wrote Thomas Wotton in 1741, 'built by the late Sir William Ellys, Bart.' It was his son Sir Richard who formed the celebrated library, now at Blickling. After his death Nocton went to Sir Francis Dashwood of West Wycombe (who married his widow), then to his mother's cousin, the 3rd Earl of Buckinghamshire. The 4th Earl's daughter married Lord Goderich. Sir William's 'beautiful seat' was burnt down in 1834, to be replaced by the present rather gloomy house built by Lord Ripon in 1841, which until recently served as an RAF Hospital.

Normanby-by-Spital An early church, with a Norman tower and notable Norman north arcade to the nave – the south arcade Early English, with stiff leaf capitals. With its Perpendicular clerestory, it is a lofty interior. The village is more or less one with Owmby, and the church is in the care of the Redundant Churches Fund.

Normanby-le-Wold Indeed at the top of the Wold, on the top of the world – with magnificent views for those climbing the hill from Claxby, and a remarkable vista from the churchyard for those who reach it.

Outwardly the church appears all by Fowler (1868), except for the early tower with its pinnacled Perpendicular top – but inside it is the medieval building, with unusual fourteenth-century nave arcades, the capitals adorned with an odd horn motif. The chancel is by Fowler, with admirable Victorian sanctuary and reredos, and panels of sixteenth-century Continental glass in the east window.

Normanton The little church presides over the small stone village in pretty Kesteven countryside – and is of architectural interest on account of its Transitional and Early English nave arcades, its distinguished embattled Perpendicular clerestory, and its good Elizabethan and modern furnishings. It is now in the care of the Redundant Churches Fund.

North Carlton Beneath the Cliff, a little church with a Perpendicular tower, the rest a charming Georgian box of 1771. Inside there is a coved ceiling, an apsidal sanctuary, a couple of small seventeenth-century brasses to Monsons, and an eighteenth-century font and altar rail. The Hall is a gabled Elizabethan Monson house.

North Carlton: the Georgian church with its medieval tower

North Coates is nowhere near Great Coates or Little Coates, and indeed is south of them both. Church rebuilt by James Fowler in 1865, but incorporating parts of the original building (*e.g.* the Early English arcades). The tower with its unusual octagonal top and pyramid roof bears that unmistakable, confident, 1860s look. A lane to the east leads to a lonely stretch of seashore.

North Elkington A tiny hamlet: S. S. Teulon has been unfortunate in these parts, for here his little church (1851) has been converted into a house, and a notice at the gate announces that those wishing to visit family graves must make written application to do so.

North Hykeham Suburban Lincoln: rows of bungalows and small houses. The church is of 1858, by Michael Drury in the Decorated style – a small, rock-faced Victorian building.

North Kelsey Remote forgotten countryside below the Wolds near Caistor. The church has an ancient tower, but the rest was largely rebuilt in 1869; some ancient fragments.

North Kyme The Skegness road roars through North Kyme, and there is but a small brick church of 1877 (by Drury and Mortimer) and an old cross in the centre of the village.

North Ormsby A tiny hillside community on the edge of the Wolds – a large farmhouse, and farm cottages. S. S. Teulon's attractive little church (1848) is now (1988) in process of conversion into a house.

North Owersby A village in remote countryside, with a little church rebuilt in 1762 of ancient materials. A narrow tower with pyramid roof; 'Lombardised' windows of 1888.

North Rauceby The church is one of the very best in this famous district, with Early English broach spire, Decorated nave with Perpendicular clerestory, chancel rebuilt by Teulon (1853) – all of outstanding quality. The village is set against the backcloth of the park of Rauceby Hall, a substantial Gothic house by Burn (1843), for the Willson family, Sleaford bankers.

North Reston Between the Wolds and the Marsh. The small church is the result of R. J. Wither's restoration of 1868: in origin medieval, there is much Norman masonry; but in the eighteenth century the little building was Georgianised, before being medievalised again by Withers.

North Scarle A charming church, on the very frontier of Notts – mostly a rebuilding of the fourteenth century, after a fire of 1342, but retaining a few fragments of its Norman and Early English predecessor. But what makes the church is the work (1895-98) of Sir Ninian Comper: his is the north aisle, together with the delightful painted ceilings, furnishings and stained glass; to him, too, are due the beautiful altars with their embroidered hangings and ornaments. Comper was always the artist.

North Somercotes A large village of cottages and bungalows, and much infilling, not far from the sea. The church lies to the south-west, down a long lane, and is easily missed. It is a large Marshland church, with Early English tower, and spacious nave of six bays. There was much

North Rauceby: Early English broach spire

rebuilding in the seventeenth century, and much restoration in the nineteenth. The most notable feature is the Perpendicular font, with carved panels of the Resurrection, emblems of the Passion, the lilies of France, the lion of Scotland, and so on.

North Thoresby A large village with much new housing. The church is hidden away at the north end, a building predominantly Early English, but with Decorated and Perpendicular additions. There is a window showing Queen Victoria in all majesty, with orb and sceptre: some visiting Poles were heard to say that they had never seen a representation of Our Lady quite like that. There are benchends of the early sixteenth century, adorned with initials (of the donors?) and other decoration.

North Willingham Here the Wolds come tumbling down in grassy knolls, and the main road climbs the steep escarpment on its way to Louth. The church is late eighteenth century, of greenstone, attached to a solid square medieval tower; Venetian east window; west gallery.

North Witham A stone village close to the infant River Witham, and a church with a delicate Perpendicular spire, and early Norman chancel arch. The long chancel opens up into what is virtually the mausoleum of the Sherard family, the altar being close to the chancel arch. There is a grand display of splendid monuments of the eighteenth-century, by Stanton and Horsnaile, Edward Sharpe of Stamford, and others. The Sherards, baronets extinct, lived at Lobthorpe in this parish, a house which has also disappeared.

Northorpe At the back of beyond: the church appears Perpendicular without – but within there are two impressive Norman arcades, and an Early English chancel. Sixteenth-and seventeenth-century brass inscriptions to Monsons; Victorian Hall (1875) with the ruinous fragment of the sixteenth-century house in the garden.

Norton Disney A romantic spot, lost in the willows of the River Witham, and surrounded by woods. The village was once dominated by the castle of the Disneys, who took their name from Isigney near Bayeux; the last of this line was executed in 1665, but their name lives on in the creator of Mickey Mouse, a descendant of a junior branch. A perfect village church of many dates, with a splendid set of tombs and brasses of the Disneys, old floors, benches, screens, Communion rails. There is

OPPOSITE *Sherard monuments at North Witham*

Norton Disney

an important brass to William Disney (1580) and his family – a palimp-sest on a hinged frame, on the back of which is a Flemish inscription, of which the other half is at West Lavington in Wiltshire.

Old Bolingbroke 'To Mavis Enderby and Old Bolingbroke' announces the signpost on the main road – to which a wag once (according to a letter in *The Times*) suspended a further notice 'A son, both doing well'.

Henry IV was born at Bolingbroke – 'Henry of Bolingbroke' – and it was a royal castle until after the Battle of Winceby (1643). Astonishing excavations have taken place in recent years, and it is now possible to get a good idea of what the castle looked like. The church is but a grand fragment of the beautiful Decorated church built by John of Gaunt, with lofty nave arcades and traceried windows. Perpendicular north-west tower; north aisle and general restoration by Fowler (1890).

Old Leake

Old Leake A magnificent church. Walk round the outside, and survey its many features: a solid Perpendicular tower, a lofty clerestoried nave with canopied niches between each of its six windows, the ornate parapet of the nave gable – then the chancel with its big traceried windows, and another elaborately carved open parapet. This is distinguished Decorated work, and, inside, the nave has six-bay Decorated arcades, which unexpectedly retain parts of a previous Norman nave; the chancel is also long and spacious. The beautiful furnishings include an eighteenth-century pulpit, an ancient alms box, and a Victorian tiled reredos.

Old Somerby A stone village with a church at the end of a cul-de-sac, facing the pleasant façade of the Old Rectory. The tower and south arcade are Early English, but there is a Norman chancel arch, and a

Perpendicular clerestory. There is a fourteenth-century effigy of a knight, and a very pretty monument (perhaps by William Stanton) to Dame Elizabeth Brownlow (1684) of Humby (*q.v.*), where the Brownlows then lived. Victorian reredos by W. A. H. Thorold (see Stainby).

Old Woodhall The mother of that delectable watering spot, Woodhall Spa. A handful of cottages, a large farm, and the site of the old church – an interesting little building of greenstone and brick, wantonly destroyed twenty or so years ago. It had a remarkable west end, with buttresses carrying a small west window, and above that an arch bearing the little bellcote and spire. Two miles south-west, against a background of Waterloo Wood, planted from acorns sown 'immediately after the memorable Battle of Waterloo', stands an obelisk bearing a bust of the Duke of Wellington, erected by Colonel Elmhirst of West Ashby, who had been one of Wellington's officers at the battle.

Orby An attractive village on the edge of the Marsh, with a clerestoried Perpendicular church of greenstone; brick fifteenth-century south porch; well-furnished interior.

Ormsby, North see **North Ormsby**

Ormsby, South see **South Ormsby**

Osbournby The wide street opens up into a broad square, lined with stone and brick and pantiled houses; the church is at the east end. It has a severe tower, and is almost entirely Decorated, with arcades and many traceried windows of this date, a beautiful sedilia, a wealth of old pews with poppyheads – and a Perpendicular north aisle.

Owersby, North see **North Owersby**

Owmby An ancient church, with Norman tower, open at its base to serve as a porch: wide views across the quiet countryside. Inside, the nave is late Norman or earliest Early English, with rough-hewn capitals and arches; Early English chancel, the whole charming and beautifully kept in an unsophisticated way. The Decorated traceried east window of the north aisle is quaintly all askew.

Owston Ferry The village street descends to the Trent, and there are wide views over the river; it is all rather Dutch in character. The church stands alone at the top of the street, and at first sight, with its tower, appears all Perpendicular; but the north side is a rebuilding in white brick of 1840, and the interior is attractive with early nineteenth-century Gothic embellishments – baptistery, sanctuary, nave roof, monuments, and early nineteenth-century stained glass. Rood screen of 1897.

Oxcombe One of the most beautiful valleys in the Wolds: fields, woodlands, a handful of cottages, and Oxcombe House. House and church were built by W. A. Nicholson in the early 1840s. The church is tiny, with a little octagonal tower surmounted by an iron coronet of pinnacles which – as Jack Yates put it – gives it 'the appearance of a startled hare'. Inside there are box pews, and monuments to the Grant family, with moving poems. The church is now in the care of the Lincolnshire Old Churches Trust.

Panton The recent history of Panton Church is a disgrace to the diocese: this modest Georgian church was wonderfully done up in 1905 by the late Christopher Turnor (of Panton Hall and Stoke Rochford – *q.v.*), himself a connoisseur, in memory of his uncle. The west door was of bronze, the pews were inlaid with mother-of-pearl, the pulpit with panels of metal, and there were medallions of Flemish glass in the windows: it was a little masterpiece of the Art Nouveau. After the Second World War this beautiful and indeed unique church was shamefully abandoned, and an attempt to rescue it by the Friends of Friendless Churches was fought off. The building was sold for use as a barn. It is a miserable story.

   Panton Hall, a notable and important work of Hawksmoor and John Carr, was demolished in the early 1960s. The Philistine has carried all before him here in Panton.

Partney The church stands at the crossroads, where two main roads meet – its greenstone Perpendicular tower with its gay galleon weather vane standing sentinel. Externally the church looks Victorian (restoration by C. E. Giles, 1862), but inside Decorated and Perpendicular arcades survive. The chancel is of 1828 (and brick). Much Victorian stained glass.

Pickworth A marvellous church in the unfrequented countryside of the Stone Belt – almost entirely Decorated, with a broach spire, and an 'unrestored' interior, with old pews, a seventeenth-century two-decker pulpit, eighteenth-century altar rails, and a fourteenth-century screen of the most delicate workmanship. The figure of an early fifteenth-century (headless) female saint still stands on its corbel, and there are beautifully furnished chapels. Above all, there are important fourteenth-century wall paintings, discovered in 1950: the Doom is over the chancel arch, and on the nave south wall figures are sizzling in a cauldron; but

Pickworth: south aisle and (right) the medieval screen and wall paintings

opposite is the friendly figure of St Christopher, and, nearby, the Ascending Christ.

Pilham Who ever visits Pilham? It is a diminutive place, worth a visit: the tiny Georgian church has an odd little tower, an apsidal sanctuary, and comfortable pews.

Pinchbeck A large leafy Fen village, the surrounding countryside gay with daffodils and tulips in spring. The church is of considerable splendour, with grand Perpendicular west tower, and an exterior largely Perpendicular – but there is earlier work inside, where, despite the Perpendicular clerestory, the arcades of the long nave are Early English, varied and interesting, with some Norman fragments incorporated. There are splendid roofs throughout, and many tombs and monuments. Butterfield rebuilt the chancel in 1856, and here there is notable Victorian decoration; there is also much good Victorian glass, including a west window by O'Connor. Altogether, a remarkable and colourful interior. Next door, the eighteenth-century rectory and stables form a delightful group, and there are several good houses of mellow brick in the village.

At West Pinchbeck Butterfield built the church in 1850 – a decent Victorian chapel-of-ease.

Pinchbeck: angels and arches

Ponton, Great see **Great Ponton**

Ponton, Little see **Little Ponton**

Potter Hanworth *Potter* Hanworth on acccount of the potteries established here by the Romans; the church was rebuilt by R. C. Hussey to replace a Georgian building, then disapproved of. But the tower is medieval, with Hussey's decorative open parapet to crown it.

Quadring One of the many grand churches near Spalding, with a finely proportioned Perpendicular tower and spire, and a Perpendicular nave with a sequence of big clerestory windows; there is a notable entrance to the rood loft close to the chancel arch. But the interior has been scraped, and there is dull modern glass of 1900 and later.

Quadring

Quarrington New houses line the main road out of Sleaford, but something is left of the old village round the church. This is chiefly Early English and Decorated, with a Decorated tower and recessed spire. The apsidal chancel is an addition of 1862.

Raithby *(near Louth)* An enchanting spot, with a church of 1839 by W. A. Nicholson – reminiscent of his church at Haugham, and equally attractive. It is of brick, cemented, and with its pinnacles and crockets and traceried parapets is fun in a way that the more serious-minded Victorian architects failed to achieve. Inside it is the same, with much of its original furnishing and colourful enamelled glass – and a barrel organ. The north arcade, incidentally, is genuine medieval work. Lovely setting of old farm buildings, trees and streams.

Raithby *(near Spilsby)* A pretty Wold village, with an eighteenth-century Hall; the church was largely rebuilt by Sir G. G. Scott in 1873, and is pleasant enough in a Victorian way. Of greater interest is the chapel, established in the Hall stable yard by Robert Carr Brackenbury, then Squire of Raithby, for John Wesley in 1779. This is charming – an upper room fitted out with pulpit and other original furnishings, and still in use.

Ranby A stone's throw from the High Street, the glorious empty road which runs along the spine of the Wolds from Caistor to Horncastle: a little aisleless church with a tower, in the Decorated style, rebuilt by Fowler in very fine ashlar in 1861; Fowler at his earliest, most restrained. Wonderful views from the churchyard.

Rand A turning off the A158 (Lincoln to Wragby) announces RAND – a tiny scattered hamlet, with a church by itself in a farmyard. It is an odd, long, low building, largely Victorian, memorable for its monuments. There are two early tombs (twelfth century), and a number of later monuments (Elizabethan or Jacobean) to the family of Fulnetby of Fulnetby, a hamlet in the parish, and to the Metham family; a seventeenth-century monument to Sir Sapcote Harington (1630), and a number of brasses. Altogether a wonderful feast for the genealogist.

Rasen, Middle see **Middle Rasen**

Rasen, West see **West Rasen**

Rauceby, North see **North Rauceby**

Ravendale, East see **East Ravendale**

Redbourne The long straight stretch of the Ermine Street (A15) finally bears right, and reaches Redbourne: a little toy-fort Gothick gateway (by Carr of York), surmounted by the royal lion, guards the entrance to the Hall, formerly a seat of the Dukes of St Albans, descendants of Charles II and Nell Gwyn. The church tower is immensely tall – given a top storey in the eighteenth century to provide an eye-catcher for the Hall. It is a medieval church (Decorated and Perpendicular), done up in Gothick dress, with the mausoleum of the St Albans family on the south side. Inside there is a charming plaster vault to nave and chancel, and there are several eighteenth and nineteenth-century monuments, including one to Harriet Mellon the actress, wife of the 9th Duke, and earlier ones to members of the Carter family: the 8th Duke married the Carter heiress, and inherited Redbourne. The fantastic east window is a lurid early nineteenth-century transparency of the Day of Judgement, designed by John Martin, and executed by William Collins. There is a black incised slab to Sir Gerald Sothill (1401), and an elegant eighteenth-century font. The church is now in the care of the Redundant Churches Fund.

Reepham Dormitory village near Lincoln. The church was almost entirely rebuilt in 1862 by Michael Drury. The surviving north arcade is fourteenth century.

Reston, North see **North Reston**

Reston, South see **South Reston**

Revesby is famous as the home of Sir Joseph Banks, explorer, naturalist, Fellow of the Royal Society, and drainer of the Fens. After his death the place descended to the Stanhopes (and so to the present owner), and the pretty village with its numerous *cottages ornées* is their creation. A lavish iron screen and gates guard the entrance to the deer park: beyond stands the mouldering mansion built by Burn in 1843 for J. Banks Stanhope. In recent years the family have built a new house in the park. The church is by Hodgson Fowler (1891), and is expensively dull, though the Edwardian reredos with Art Nouveau angels weeping, and mother-of-pearl inlay, is more exciting. One Banks monument, with bust, by Nost (1727).

Riby A cruciform church, standing beside a desolate park: the great house of the Tomlines and Pretymans was pulled down just before the Second World War. The church was considerably rebuilt by Benjamin Ferrey in 1868, but much medieval work survives, especially the early

Revesby: Art Nouveau angels on the reredos

fourteenth--century crossing, and Perpendicular tower. Tomline and Pretyman monuments and hatchments.

Rigsby A solitary farmhouse, and a tiny church by James Fowler (1863) in one of his more interesting moods (Neo-Norman). Views from the edge of the Wolds towards the coast.

Rippingale Travelling south along the A15 there is a wonderful view of the grand sweep of the Fens to the east, and of the rolling stone country, well wooded, to the west. There is the tapering spire of Walcot, then the tall pinnacled tower of Folkingham; Aslackby tower in its hollow comes next – then, as the country flattens out, the grand tower of Rippingale. It is Perpendicular with tall pinnacles. The church itself is chiefly Deco-rated, with a spacious nave of six bays, with big traceried windows. There is an array of exceptional medieval monuments with effigies, which speak of the importance of Rippingale in the Middle Ages.

Riseholme Riseholme Hall, now the Agricultural College, was for a time the episcopal residence: it was Bishop Kay who rebuilt the church in 1851. It is a small handsome building by S. S. Teulon in the Decorated style, lavishly decorated, the chancel richly lit with Gibbs glass.

Ropsley The largest of the villages in the stone uplands south-east of Grantham. An interesting church, with an Early English tower surmounted by a Decorated broach spire. But the nave is in origin Anglo-Saxon (long and short work), with a Norman north arcade. The south arcade is Early English, as is the chancel; Decorated clerestory. The porch is dated 1486, and above the doorway is the inscription 'Hac non vade via, nisi dicas Ave Maria', a delightful hexameter meaning 'Do not come this way, without saying an Ave Maria'.

Rothwell In a beautiful fold of the Wolds – an idyllic setting for a distinguished Anglo-Saxon tower; inside, a nave with two grand Norman arcades, and a chancel restored by Sedding in 1892, complete with his delightful furnishings. A very special church.

Roughton *(pronounced 'Rooton')* The attractive back road from Tattershall to Horncastle, overlooking the Bain. A simple church with a Perpendicular tower of brick on a greenstone base, and earlier nave and chancel, with old woodwork inside, and the fascinating monument to a non-juror: 'Here lies the body of Norreys Fynes, Esqre, grandson to Sir Henry Clinton (commonly called Fynes) . . . From the Revolution he always lived a non-juror, which rendered him incapable of any other Public Employment than that of being Steward to two great estates . . .' (died 1735). The Hall is a handsome mid-eighteenth-century house, of brick with stone dressings, with Venetian and Diocletian windows to complete a delightful façade.

Rowston A very slender, almost miniature, Early English tower and 'candle-snuffer' spire; Early English nave with Perpendicular clerestory, a Norman tympanum under the tower – all rewarding. Of special interest, however, are the Hanoverian royal arms and Commandment boards which once served as a tympanum above the chancel screen and were removed in an early twentieth-century 'restoration', and replaced with very ordinary ecclesiastical furnishings. Mercifully all the sections were preserved in the aisle or vestry, and could be replaced. It is much to be hoped that they will be. Charming early eighteenth-century stone manor house next door.

OPPOSITE *Riseholme by S.S. Teulon*

Roxby Magnificent views across the village towards the Humber with the Yorkshire hills on the far side, and that splendid white elephant, the Humber Bridge, ethereally suspended across the river. Roxby is full of bijou residences, and the churchyard denuded of its gravestones and planted in matching bijou style, alas. The church has a Saxon (or early Norman) tower, but much of the rest was rebuilt by James Fowler in 1875; it retains, however, many medieval features inside.

Ruckland A fascinating Nordic-looking little church, high on a shelf of beautiful Wold, with overhanging roof, rose window, and ancient runic cross – a work of great originality by W. Scorer, 1885. 'Very remote,' wrote Jack Yates in the *Shell Guide*: 'one can almost understand how one Victorian incumbent got into the habit of beating his wife.'

Ruskington A large towny village, with suburban villas galore. But a brook runs through the middle of the broad village street, and there are some old houses here. The church has a squat tower (a rebuilding of 1620), and, inside, a Decorated south aisle of real distinction (comparable with work at Lincoln). Some restoration by Charles Kirk: to him are due the Victorian furnishings. The east window is by Ward and Hughes – but the east window of the south aisle is one of special interest: the Ascension, by William Morris, with figures of Our Lord and two attendant angels, translucent and ethereal. A very beautiful window.

Saleby An elegant essay in Decorated Gothic by Stephen Lewin, 1850. Good rood screen and other Victorian furnishings; notable early fourteenth-century effigy in the sanctuary.

Salmonby Steps lead up the rocky path to the churchyard, where once stood a charming little greenstone church, medieval and Victorian. This was monstrously abandoned, and then even more monstrously destroyed, in 1976, though a Society of the Friends of Salmonby had been formed to take it over, and look after it. A shocking business.

Saltfleetby All Saints A compelling sight: the church long and low, with tall leaning tower, and great lead roof shining grey and white above the Marshland reeds and grasses; there is a scattering of houses and the Prussian Queen, and a dead-end lane leads to the church. The gently leaning tower appears ready to fall into the marsh, and the weighty, humpy lead roof appears to be slipping off its crown; the texture is marvellous with grey or green or brown stone, with an ample patching of old red brick. Inside, it is wonderful, too, with Early English nave, older chancel arch, ancient roofs, Perpendicular screens, two old

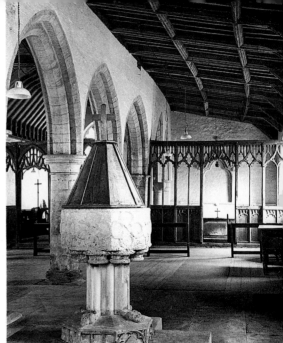

Saltfleetby All Saints: views of the interior

pulpits, and – rarest of all – a medieval stone reredos in the Lady Chapel. This precious gem among Lincolnshire churches is now in the care of the Redundant Churches Fund.

Saltfleetby St Clement The church stands by itself in the fields beside the main road, and is chiefly of 1885 (by W. Mortimer), with a plain tower, and incorporating some medieval features. Declared redundant, it is now used as a studio and workshop.

Saltfleetby St Peter The tower of the old church stands alone in the fields to the north-east. It is Perpendicular, of green and white stone, and is now in the care of the Friends of Friendless Churches. The church itself was moved, and rebuilt nearer the straggling village on the main road in 1877. Much of the old building (Early English and Decorated) was retained and re-used.

Sapperton A little church with Early English tower and diminutive spire, lost in the back lanes of the uplands south-east of Grantham; the former north arcade (Transitional or Early English) is blocked up. Two seventeenth-century monuments to the Saunders family; rood by Wilfrid Bond. The approach is charming, with the long low seventeenth-century manor house hard by.

Sausthorpe The crocketed spire, supported by flying buttresses and tall pinnacles *à la* Louth, is a prominent landmark in the Wold country – where there are but few spires. This is of 1842, by Charles Kirk, and the interior, a lofty narrow nave and short chancel, with pews and west gallery, is vintage 1842, and by no means unattractive. Late Morris glass (1908). The Old Hall opposite is a charming house – outwardly eighteenth century but in fact a much earlier building; it has a delightful garden.

Saxby All Saints A pretty village on the western slopes of the northernmost Wolds. An early church by Sir G. G. Scott (1845 *ff*), with a later tower (1873) by another hand. The Hall is a charming smaller Georgian house with bow windows.

Saxby St Helen A delightful little Georgian brick church (c. 1775), with a grand pillared portico, built by the Sandersons, Earls of Castleton (of Glentworth, *q.v.*) as their place of burial, later of their heirs and successors, the Lumleys, Earls of Scarbrough, whose monuments and hatchments adorn the interior – whose apsidal sanctuary with its coffered ceiling is a special pleasure.

Saxilby A large village on the Foss Dyke Navigation: although there is no building of note, the *tout ensemble* of the waterfront is delightful. The church lies to the north, among rows and rows and rows of boring bungalows; the north doorway is Norman, the nave arcade Early English, but the general impression is of a Perpendicular church, with large Perpendicular windows in aisle and clerestory; rood screen and twin chancel and chantry chapel, containing a tomb of c. 1400.

Scamblesby Magnificent, sweeping views of the Wold landscape, as the road (A153) dips down from the Dutch House – to rise again to Cawkwell Top. The little church with its bellcote sits on a shelf, commanding another splendid view. It is a rebuilding of 1893 by Reggie Fowler, son of the ubiquitous James, but contains a Norman pier from Cawkwell (which collapsed a century or more ago), and some old poppyheads.

Scampton The RAF station is on the Cliff, the village below. Attractive village church, mostly Perpendicular, with modest tower – all beautifully furnished and cared for. In the sanctuary a small brass to Sir John Bolle (1648); nothing remains of the Bolles' house, except for the forlorn but impressive Jacobean gateway (see also Haugh).

Scarle, North see **North Scarle**

Saxby St Helen: village Georgian

Scartho Now caught up in Grimsby suburbia – but behind the rows of bungalows stands the tall Saxon tower of the church, a splendid sight. Sympathetic enlargement of the church by T. J. Rushton (1955-8).

Scawby High old brick walls denote the presence of Scawby Hall, seat of the Nelthorpes, a rambling house of the seventeenth and eighteenth centuries with gables and tall chimneys. The church has a medieval tower; the rest is by W. A. Nicholson (1843), comparable with his church at Brigg, curiously towny, with thin Gothic details – of interest for the series of Nelthorpe monuments and hatchments which it contains.

Scopwick A pretty village, with a stream running through: were this the Cotswolds, tourists would come flocking – but this is Lincolnshire, dull, flat, boring Lincolnshire, so no one comes, thank God. The church was much restored in the mid nineteenth century, but the tower is Early English below, seventeenth century above, with domestic-looking bell openings, and plain parapet. Inside, there are Early English arcades and an effigy of a fourteenth-century knight.

Scot Willoughby A little hamlet in pretty country, off the Bridge End Road: a tiny church of 1826, Gothic, and incorporating material from the medieval church; seventeenth-century pulpit, eighteenth-century altar rails.

Scothern The pinnacled tower is Perpendicular – but the nave was rebuilt in 1796, and is a big plain box, with Victorian Gothic windows inserted; the chancel arch is medieval, but the chancel was rebuilt in 1904. All this sounds unpromising, but it is in fact an attractive, well-furnished church.

Scotter Once a market town, now but a fair-sized village of red-brick cottages, with the tall tower of the church presiding. The tower is Perpendicular, as is the clerestory, but a Norman south doorway leads in to a distinguished Early English nave arcade. It is a sparkling white interior, with some box pews, Perpendicular font and screen, and two small brasses.

Scotton Wide views here – from the valley of the Trent towards the Cliff. A plain Decorated tower with Perpendicular top, Early English and Decorated arcades, Decorated chancel – but two Norman doorways; the light, spacious interior contains four notable fourteenth-century tombs, and a font by Street (1866).

Scredington Gentle countryside on the edge of the Fens. The church is medieval in origin, but much rebuilt in 1869. It has a very odd, tall tapering needle spire, perched on an equally odd polygonal low tower.

Scremby From the road below a good sight: a Georgian church on the hill, in the middle of parkland. And on your climbing the hill it will not disappoint. It was built in 1733, of brick with stone dressings. Inside there is a Snetzler organ, a west gallery, a Venetian east window, and a comfortable array of pews and period furnishings. A beautiful landscape, with views across the great Fen.

Scrivelsby The Lion Gate stands at the entrance to the Park: there are glades of beech trees, and deer. Almost invisible from the road stands the home of the Dymokes, to whom since the fourteenth century has fallen the right to act as Queen's Champion at the Coronation.

The church stands across the road in a field against a backcloth of woods. It is largely a Victorian restoration (1860) of the medieval church; the small steeple is of this date. Inside, the arcade is thirteenth century – but the great thing is the display of monuments to the Champions. There are effigies of early knights (c. 1300), probably Marmions from whom the Dymokes inherited, and the distinguished tomb, with brass inset, to Sir Robert Dymoke (1545), together with later monuments to successive Champions. The east window is by Willement.

Scunthorpe is not an attractive place: how could it be? It is a large industrial town which grew up suddenly at the end of the last century on the discovery of iron ore in the district. The great steel works dominate the scene, and the centre of the town is drab, with long uninteresting streets built in the brightest of red brick.

The former parish church of St John (1889 by Crowther), with its grand Perpendicular tower, is stately but bleak. Moreover it was built in the wrong place, surrounded by factories and warehouses; it is now redundant, its windows boarded up, its future uncertain. The ancient mother church is St Laurence, Frodingham, and this is now the parish church of Scunthorpe. It is a good medieval building, Early English, Decorated and Perpendicular, and to it in 1913 Sir Charles Nicholson added a new nave and chancel on the north side, in his own characteristic, sympathetic style, Gothic but original.

His partner, H. C. Corlette, built in 1924 two new churches (consecratd on the same day) – St Paul's Ashby, and St George's, Crosby, both of brick with stone dressings, in a pleasant 1920s Gothic taste. Both are,

Sedgebrook: benchend angel. RIGHT *Silk Willoughby.*

as yet, unfinished. St Hugh's Old Brumby was completed in 1939, and is a successful and original building in concrete and brick by Lawrence Bond.

In recent years some attempt has been made at imaginative town planning, with a large central park (near St Laurence Church), in which has been built the new Civic Centre, a museum and a theatre. Scunthorpe is being spruced up.

Searby Charmingly set on the side of the Wolds, a little church of white brick built in 1832, with tower and apse and – inside – west gallery, and elaborate screen and stalls carved by a Victorian incumbent. Two handsome early nineteenth-century monuments in the sanctuary by Earle of Hull.

Sedgebrook A church of great distinction, built of silvery Ancaster stone and golden ironstone, almost all Perpendicular and of splendid proportions – where the sunlight pours into a spacious glistening-white interior, picking out ancient screens, chancel stalls, pulpit, and carved stone niches in the lofty chancel. The north nave arcade survives from the earlier church; the great rebuilding was due to Sir John Markham, the judge, in 1468. Next door is the manor house, with its distinguished façade built in the early eighteenth century by Sir John Thorold, masking the much earlier house built by the Markhams.

Sempringham A holy place: here St Gilbert founded the only English monastic Order, the Gilbertines. St Gilbert, son of a wealthy Norman knight, was born here in (probably) 1083. The great monastic church, and all the monastic buildings, lay to the south, marked now only by a few bumps in the grass. The lonely church across the fields from the main road is the church built by St Gilbert's father, and the church in which the Order was founded, the village church, except that there is no village. It is a building of beauty and romance, with its Norman nave and Norman south doorway (with early thirteenth-century door with contemporary ironwork); the central tower is Perpendicular, the small apsidal chancel Victorian (by E. Browning, 1869). St Gilbert died in 1189, and was canonised in 1202.

Sibsey A very grand medieval Fen church, with lofty tower – Early English its lower stages with beautiful paired bell openings, and a Perpendicular battlemented top. The nave is clerestoried, and the tall arcades with Norman capitals, their piers curiously elongated in the fourteenth century, give the interior the look of an early Christian basilica. An attractive village, with a number of seventeenth-and eight-eenth-century houses, and a windmill in full working order.

Silk Willoughby The A15 makes tortuous twists and turns through the village: the splendid Decorated spire of the church stands calm and unconcerned above all this – with its parapet, pinnacles and flying buttresses. The Decorated nave is spacious – with poppyhead pews, rood screen and Jacobean pulpit.

Sixhills The church with its pinnacled tower and apsidal east end was almost entirely rebuilt by James Fowler in 1869. A sequestered, pretty spot, with memories of a Gilbertine priory founded here c. 1150.

Skegness 'Skegness is so bracing': the famous advertisement for the place, with a jolly fisherman dancing along the beach, says everything. 'A pleasant village and bathing place,' says William White in his *Direc-tory* (1843) '. . . it has several private lodging houses, and two large and commodious hotels.' The place developed into a large seaside town during the nineteenth century, under the aegis of the Earls of Scar-brough, the landowners – just as Folkestone did under the Earls of Radnor, Littlehampton under the Dukes of Norfolk, and Eastbourne under the Dukes of Devonshire. Skegness became the great seaside metropolis for the Midlands. The old village church stands inland, now surrounded by suburban housing, with a low medieval tower and fifteenth-century aisleless nave and chancel, all patched with brick. St

Matthew's is the new church of the seaside town, by James Fowler (1879 *ff*) and Bassett Smith, with bellcote and apsidal chancel.

Skellingthorpe Villas and larger houses are growing up in the woods that accompany the road from Lincoln: there is little 'village'. The church of 1885 (by Kendall and Pope), with the adjoining school, forms a pleasant group, though the nave of the former is still in the patched-up state it has been in since a fire in 1915. The most interesting thing is the grand tomb on the edge of the churchyard 'erected by the Governors of Christ's Hospital, London, to their benefactor Henry Stone, Esqre' – a splendid work of 1693.

Skendleby Beautiful Wold countryside. The church stands in a pretty setting, and is in origin medieval, but Sir G. G. Scott's restoration of 1875 makes it appear largely Victorian. A good Perpendicular font.

Skidbrook In the Middle Ages Saltfleet Haven was an important port: now it is but a small village lurking behind the sea bank. Skidbrook Church stands more than a mile away, quite alone across dyked fields, in majestic isolation. Green with moss, it has spacious fourteenth-century nave, with aisles, chancel and tower. Abandoned for many years, it is all textured like a deserted church in Tuscany, but is now being cared for by the Redundant Churches Fund, and its future is assured.

Skillington A stone village on the Leicestershire frontier. The church contains Saxon fragments, but is chiefly Early English and Decorated, with a well-proportioned Decorated broach spire. Of special interest is the window in memory of the Revd Charles Hudson, then vicar of the parish, who lost his life on the Matterhorn in 1865.

Sleaford It is a pleasure to stand in the Market Place and survey the west front of the parish church, pinnacled and niched, traceried and moulded. To its left, and half hidden, is the vicarage, partly Elizabethan, partly Victorian; the restrained Tudor Gothic Sessions House (by H. E. Kendall, 1831) faces the church, and all around are pleasant Georgian houses, such as the Old Bristol Arms, now converted into a shopping arcade. A litle farther on is Carre's Hospital, rebuilt by Kendall in 1836: from its charming open Gothic quadrangle there is a grand view of the church with its breathtaking series of enormous Decorated traceried windows.

But stand before the west front of the church: the broach spire is one of the earliest of all English stone spires (late twelfth – early thirteenth

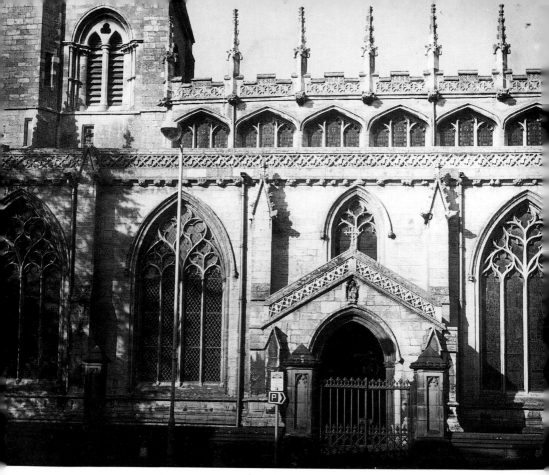

Sleaford

century). The nave is Decorated, the lofty arches supported on slender pillars, and all around are the magnificent traceried windows. The nave clerestory and the chancel are Perpendicular. Between them stands the Perpendicular rood screen, which Pugin described as one of the most perfect in England; the rood itself and figures are by Comper. The rails before the high altar are seventeenth century, and were originally in Lincoln Cathedral.

The Carre monuments range from the brass to George Carre (1521) to the marble bust of Sir Edward (1683): they include one by Maximilian Colt (1618). The Carres were the great benefactors of Sleaford, founding the Grammar School (1604), and Carre's Hospital (1630).

Snarford In the middle of nowhere – a farmhouse, and a handful of cottages, and a small church apparenty of little consequence. But the door opens into an interior of theatrical excitement. There are pews, and

there is an altar – but the whole building is dominated by huge Elizabethan and Jacobean tombs. Behind the altar, occupying the whole chancel, is the canopied tomb of Sir Thomas and Lady St Paul (1582), and in the chapel another to Sir George (1613), his wife (née Frances Wray), and their daughter. Next to it, a monument with medallion portraits to this Frances Wray and her second husband, Robert Rich, Earl of Warwick (1619); they look out at us from the wall like faces in a carriage window. There are other smaller memorials. The family, their wealth, their descendants are vanished – and there is now only the farmhouse on the site of their once great house.

Snelland On the back road between Lincoln and Market Rasen: only the railway occasionally disturbs its peace. Edward Browning almost rebuilt the church in 1863; a few medieval fragments survive.

Snitterby The church was rebuilt by James Fowler in 1866, with west tower and east apse. Inside it is unexpectedly all lined in brick – red, yellow, black; indeed it is vintage Fowler throughout.

Somerby *(near Brigg)* The little church with its low tower stands on the slopes of the wooded Wold – a medieval building much patched up in the seventeenth and eighteenth centuries; thirteenth-century effigy of a knight, with his puppy and a lion at his feet; monument to Sir Edward Rossiter, the Parliamentarian, and eighteenth-century tablets to the Westons who built the Georgian Hall, recently demolished. An obelisk in the park still stands, erected by Edward Weston in 1770, to celebrate twenty-nine years of a happy marriage; Stephen Weston, Lower Master of Eton and Bishop of Exeter, was of this family.

Somerby, Old see **Old Somerby**

Somercotes, North see **North Somercotes**

Somercotes, South see **South Somercotes**

Somersby Anybody who has read Sir Charles Tennyson's *Alfred Tennyson* will be familiar with the story, how the Revd George Tennyson, the poet's father, came to be rector here in 1806, having been passed over by his father for the family property at Bayons Manor, which went instead to his younger brother, who was thought more likely to promote the glory of the Tennyson family. George was forced to take Holy Orders, a calling for which he felt unsuited, and which throughout his life he found uncongenial. Yet it was his son who made the name Tennyson immortal. Alfred Tennyson was born here in 1809.

OPPOSITE *Elizabethan and Jacobean tombs at Snarford (John Piper)*

The little medieval church, of greenstone patched with brick, contains a bust of Tennyson and many souvenirs of interest. The former rectory, now a private residence and not open to the public, stands opposite, cream-washed and charming. Next door is a house of particular fascination, built of mellow red brick, castellated, with corner turrets and round-headed windows, so Vanbrughesque that it is often ascribed to Vanbrugh. The village lies in a particularly beautiful hollow of the Wolds, watered by the brook.

Sotby On the edge of the Wolds. An enormous churchyard with magnificent views, and a modest little medieval church, somewhat rebuilt in the eighteenth century; Georgian windows, Norman chancel arch.

South Carlton Under the Cliff north of Lincoln: a dead-end village of farms and cottages, church and manor house. The church is medieval, but much rebuilt by Teulon in 1860. His is the wide slate roof, decorated

South Carlton: a medieval church restored by S.S. Teulon

South Cockerington: monument to Sir Adrian Scrope

in his characteristic way with bands of different-coloured slates. Inside, the arcades are ancient, and there is a Perpendicular screen, a number of old seats, a curious rectangular Victorian pulpit, a gay little Victorian organ, and a splendid tomb by Nicholas Stone of Sir John and Lady Monson (1625); the walls are hung with Monson hatchments. The manor house, next door, has a charming early eighteenth-century front, concealing a fragment of a much earlier house, the ancient home of the Monsons, one of Lincolnshire's oldest families. In recent years Lord Monson and his family have returned (from Burton, *q.v.*) to live here.

South Cockerington A Perpendicular church with bold west tower, and a wide aisleless interior of Marshland character. The figure of Sir Adrian Scrope – 'thrice noble knight' – half reclining as though rising from his bed, dominates the interior, a handsome monument, attributed to Epiphanius Evesham. The Hall, home of the Scropes, demolished in 1921, stood in the sad, overgrown, walled garden east of the church.

South Elkington A pretty spot in the Wolds near Louth: the village street leads up to the church, which is in origin medieval, but partially rebuilt in 1843, and again in 1873: the Perpendicular tower and thirteenth-century arcades are original. It stands in a beautifully kept churchyard, looking across to the park with its Victorian plantations. Only a fragment of the house survives – built of white brick by W. A. Nicholson in 1841 for the Smyth family: a former squire had the distinction (early this century) of roller-skating from John o' Groats to London.

South Ferriby The long meandering road (B1204) from Brigg to the Humber reaches South Ferriby: it is an exciting moment, with the first glimpse of the Humber below. The church is perched above: 'a singular structure,' remarks Kelly, 'a mutilated remnant of a much larger church'. Exactly. There are Norman fragments built into a much later building, with a Norman tympanum in the porch, and an eighteenth-century brick tower; the chancel is by Hodgson Fowler (1889).

South Hykeham survives as a village, but only the spire of the church is ancient (fourteenth century). The rest of the building was early eighteenth-century, but all Gothicised by Michael Drury in 1869 – plain, Victorian, apsidal.

South Kelsey The much-weathered tower is fourteenth century: the rest of the church was rebuilt in 1795, but Gothicised by Butterfield in 1853. It is of interest on account of the early fourteenth-century effigy of Robert Hansard, and the fifteenth-century brasses of Sir Richard Hansard and his wife. The moated site and fragments of the fifteenth-century house of the family survive south of the village.

South Kyme is wonderful, remote, treed, watered – a great tower standing by itself, relic of the castle of the Kymes and Umfravilles. The church nearby is all that remains of a grand priory of Augustinian canons, founded here in the mid-twelfth century, restored by Hodgson Fowler in 1890. There is an imposing Norman doorway (give the door a good push), and inside there are some Anglo-Saxon fragments. There are two delightful Georgian farmhouses in the background – otherwise all is silence. A place not to be missed.

South Ormsby The Massingberd Arms, the Park, and across the Park James Paine's house, home of the Massingberd-Mundys. The church stands to the south on the hillside. It has an imposing Perpendicular tower – the rest of the church is Early English and Decorated, though James Fowler had his hand in 1871. There are three notable brasses, two to Skipwiths, and later monuments to the Massingberds, medallions of Flemish glass, an east window by Clayton and Bell, and a notable fifteenth-century font. Beautiful Wold countryside.

South Reston James Fowler's small, rock-faced apsidal church of 1864 – perfect for a small community – was conveniently condemned as a 'dangerous structure' a few years ago, and destroyed. Pathetic.

South Somercotes Dykes, and Marshland scenery. The church is the 'Queen of the Marsh', and worthy of the name. Decorated tower and tapering recessed spire; spacious Early English nave of five bays – an unrestored, unsophisticated interior. Perpendicular screen; important Perpendicular font, carved with the emblems of the Passion. Now in the care of the Redundant Churches Fund.

South Thoresby A tiny village in a leafy valley: a little brick church of 1735, and a former rectory of 1853 by S. S. Teulon, with a skilful display of gables and chimneys in variegated brick. The church has a pinnacled tower and Venetian east window, but has lost much of its original furnishing.

South Willingham At the end of a grassy walk, a churchyard with wide spreading views across beautiful Wold country; there is a Perpendicular tower with a clock in the embattled parapet, an aisleless Gothic nave of 1838, and a medieval chancel. Inside, a Perpendicular screen (with restored top), and an interesting fourteenth-century font with square bowl on a shafted base.

South Witham A large village, close to the source of the River Witham, close to the Rutland frontier. A modest, but not uninteresting church of the twelfth and thirteenth centuries, with a double bellcote. The chancel collapsed in the sixteenth century, and was rebuilt in 1930 to the design of Wifrid Bond.

Southrey A decayed little ferry, where the River Witham bends and broadens on its journey from Lincoln to the Wash; the railway used to follow the river here for miles – in 1965 the station was still open, lit by oil lamps. Now all is gone. But the charming white-painted wooden church (1898) is still open, looking like a mission church in the colonies

Southrey: the wooden church

– though, alas, it has lost its enormous weathercock which used to grace its cupola.

Spalding is a Dutch-like town, with the River Welland in a deep tidal channel running through the centre like a street. Delightful brick houses, terraces and old warehouses line its banks. The Dutch character has been accentuated during this century by the introduction of bulb growing: the bulb fields in spring are well worth a visit.

There are a number of grand houses in the town – such as eighteenth-century Holland House; the most historic is Ayscoughee Hall near the parish church, originally Tudor, but overlaid in fanciful early nineteenth-century Gothick, once the home of the great Maurice John-son, and generations of his family, and now a museum. The medieval parish church is of many dates, and of great interest – founded (we know from records) in 1284. The earliest parts are the chancel with its lancet windows, and the lower stages of the tower, which stands at the north-west corner. The church is almost as wide as it is long, which gives it its special character. The main body of the building is Deco-rated, with lofty nave and aisles, and north and south transepts. In the fourteenth century the outer aisles were added, the upper part of the tower, and the spire with its crocketed pinnacles and flying buttresses. The north porch must have followed soon after, with its fan-vaulted roof. Gilbert Scott added the north chapel at his restoration in 1867; the

Spalding: SS Mary and Nicolas (John Piper, Tate Archive)

rood screen is by Oldrid Scott (1875); there is much glass by Clayton and Bell, and a number of monuments to the Johnson family of Ayscoughee Hall, with their accompanying hatchments. It is a beautifully furnished, atmospheric interior.

St John's is by R. J. Withers (1875), a stone church, externally of no special note, but, inside, a delightfully furnished and devotional building. St Paul's, by Gilbert Scott (1880), may seem frightening externally on account of its glaring red brick, but it is a building of considerable grandeur, and its design inside, with its unusual feature of double arches for each span of the arcade, must be copied from Boxgrove Priory and Portsmouth Cathedral.

The learned Spalding Gentlemen's Society was founded in 1710 by Maurice Johnson, and among its distinguished members it has numbered Newton, Pope, Addison, Stukeley and Hans Sloane. It still flourishes.

Spilsby A long Market Place, presided over by the statue of Sir John Franklin, the awe-inspiring Doric portico of the Sessions House, the long and ancient avenue to Eresby, the parish church at the crossroads: Spilsby is an engaging little hilltop town, the pinnacled tower of the church a landmark across the Wolds.

The church is somewhat forbidding outside with its rock-faced walls, owing to Bassett Smith's vigorous restoration and enlargement in 1879 – though the tower retains its original attractive greenstone. Inside there appear to be four parallel naves – Bassett Smith added an extra south aisle – but two of the arcades are fourteenth century. The chancel is also fourteenth century, but everything is somewhat over-restored. However, it is the Willoughby tombs that everybody comes to see, and these are in the Willoughby Chapel. They are a magnificent set, ranging from John, 1st Lord Willoughby de Eresby (1348) to Peregrine, 10th Lord (1601) and his daughter (1610); there are alabaster effigies, brasses, the very unusual reredos-like tomb of Richard Bertie (1582) and his wife, Baroness Willoughby de Eresby, and the more conventional Jacobean tomb to the 10th Lord and his daughter. And the series continues at Edenham (*q.v.*).

The avenue to Eresby runs straight from the town to the site of the Willoughbys' ancient house – though now rudely cut in half by the new by-pass (A16). It was burnt in 1769, and never rebuilt: Grimsthorpe had already supplanted it as their chief seat. But one solitary great seventeenth-century gatepier still stands to mark the site, capped by a grandiloquent urn.

Spilsby: detail of tomb of Peregrine 10th Lord Willoughby de Eresby and his daughter

Spital A plain little chapel, by the roadside (A15) – with traffic rushing past along the Ermine Street; rebuilt in 1616, it has mullioned windows and a little bell turret, but was originally founded in 1398 as a hospital (hence 'spital'). It is now disused, and belongs to the adjoining house (1620), which was indeed the 'spital'.

Spridlington James Fowler's church rises like a great rock above the village street: it is one of his most stately buildings, with imposing tower with saddleback roof. It was erected in 1873, to replace a small Georgian church.

Springthorpe Forgotten countryside: blue doors and gates denote a Bacon estate village (see Gainsborough). The church has a late Saxon, or early Norman, tower – the rest of the building being either genuine Norman or Norman Revival of 1845; there is a white paper funeral garland of 1814 – a rare relic.

Stainby A faded photograph in the vestry shows the church as it was before 1865: a modest building with a small tower. What we see today is due to the long incumbencies of nineteenth-century rectors. George Osborne, illegitimate son of the then Earl of Harborough, patron of the living, became rector in 1809, and refronted the handsome (former) rectory; his son rebuilt the church, an imposing building of 1865 (by R. Coad), with its grand broach spire. W. A. H. Thorold became rector in 1877, and filled the church with his carvings – altar and reredos, choir stalls, screens, organ case, pulpit and lofty font cover: everything was made in his workshop at the rectory.

Stainfield A remote spot, with a little church of 1711, old farm buildings nearby, and an early nineteenth-century farmhouse in white brick, occupying the site of the former seat of the Tyrwhitts. The church is of great charm, with its little narrow tower and lead-covered cap; the interior has been ruined by some heavy-handed Victorian. But there remain interesting panels of embroidery, worked by members of the Tyrwhitt family, and a few fragments of eighteenth-century woodwork.

Stainton by Langworth A Georgian church (1796) with a little tower with pyramid roof; inside, a monument with kneeling figures to three generations of the Sanderson family (1619) of Reesby Hall, ancestors of the Earls of Castleton (see Saxby St Helen), from whom the Earls of Scarbrough inherited so much property in Lincolnshire.

Stainton-le-Vale In a very pretty hollow of the Wolds, an ancient little

Stainfield

church of Norman and Early English origins, which has once been much larger.

Stallingborough A Georgian church of 1745 – but the interior Victorianised and empty. However, of great interest are the Ayscough monuments. There are brasses to Sir William (1541) and his wife, and an alabaster monument to Sir Edward (1612) and his wife – with his father Sir Francis above, a fascinating bust, peering out of his little arch, his head propped up on one arm, with the other holding a weapon: 'Franciscus Ayscoghe eques auratus pater infra positi Dni Edovardi.' Stallingborough Hall, home of the family, stood nearby to the north-west – but nothing remains.

Stamford is one of the two or three most beautiful towns in England. It owes its beauty to the local building stone, and its preservation to the protection of a great local family. It has had three special periods of

The broach spire of St Mary's, Stamford

All Saints', Stamford: Early English arcading on south wall

St John Baptist, Stamford: the nave roof

prosperity. The first was medieval and religious, when the earlier churches were built, and many religious orders came here to found houses, colleges and schools. The second was commercial: in the fifteenth century wealth came to the town from wool, and the Perpendicular churches were built by the wealthy wool merchants. This prosperity continued into the sixteenth century, when Queen Elizabeth granted the manor to Lord Burghley, and it is to his descendants that we owe so much for the protection of this superlative town. In the eighteenth century, with the increase of traffic on the Great North Road, Stamford became a great centre of social life: every street abounds with houses, great and small, of this period. Street follows street, and round every corner there is yet another church – with a vista of more towers and spires to follow.

There are five medieval churches. All Saints' dominates Red Lion Square with its Perpendicular tower and crocketed spire; indeed at first sight the church appears Perpendicular; but the unusual Early English blank arcading along the south wall, and the Early English arcades

St Martin's, Stamford: monument to 5th Earl of Exeter

within, betray the earlier origins of the building. There is a good
Victorian reredos, and a number of eighteenth-century monuments,
and earlier brasses – especially that to William Browne (1489), founder
of Browne's Hospital.

St John Baptist stands opposite, and is an intimate Perpendicular
church, with original angel roof, many fragments of most beautiful
contemporary glass, Perpendicular screens, eighteenth-century monuments and fifteenth-century brasses, and two fierce Victorian windows
(east and west) by Oliphant (1878).

St George's stands in St George's Square, and is in origin thirteenth
century, but the chancel was rebuilt in 1449 by Sir William Burges, first
Garter King of Arms. There are eighteenth-century monuments here,
too, notably that to Sir Richard Cust (1734) by Bacon.

St Martin's guards the entrance to the town from the south. Past the
Bottle Lodges to Burghley House is the view of High Street St Martin's
which Turner painted and Scott loved, with the west tower of the
church dominant – a Perpendicular church throughout, known to have

St Martin's, Stamford: the great Lord Burghley   *Christopher Whall's glass in St Mary's*

been built by Bishop Russell of Lincoln c. 1480. It is grand and spacious, and of exceptional interest on account of the wealth of fifteenth-century glass from Tattershall, arranged here by Peckitt of York c. 1760 – and the Cecil tombs. Here, beside the high altar, is the tomb of Lord Burghley himself (1598).

The broach spire of St Mary's stands sentinel across the river, and beckons the visitor to cross the bridge: it is undoubtedly the most magnificent broach spire in England (early fourteenth century on a thirteenth-century tower), and inside the church is of great interest too – with its high altar and rood screen by Sedding, its glass by Wailes and Christopher Whall, and the medieval tombs in the Lady Chapel with its Perpendicular 'cradle' roof; this is a beautifully furnished interior of numinous and devotional atmosphere.

In addition to the parish churches, the chapel of Browne's Hospital (in Broad Street) may be visited at certain times, with its spectacular fifteenth-century glass recently restored.

Stapleford Lost in the willowy flatness of the meadows by the Witham, a little eighteenth-century church with an ancient stone tower capped with a low pyramid roof, standing all alone up a long grassy path. A precious, simple little church.

Steeping, Great see **Great Steeping**

Steeping, Little see **Little Steeping**

Stenigot A lovely Wold valley: the little brick church of 1892, by the roadside, is outwardly unpromising, but inside there are two little alabaster monuments with kneeling figures, to Francis Velles de Guevara (1592), and Sir John Guevara (1607). The family came over from Spain with Catherine of Aragon, and prospered – but by the time of the Restoration their property had gone to the Alingtons, and the last member of the family was a hairdresser in Market Rasen.

Stewton At the end of a long lane, a tiny Norman church with primitive features – but somewhat over-restored by Reggie Fowler in 1866.

Stickford At the northern end of the vegetable belt; the church has a tall Perpendicular tower, but much of the exterior is due to James Fowler's restoration of 1881. The interior displays Early English nave arcades, but is much Victorianised.

Stickney Sibsey, Stickney and Stickford . . . a row of villages on the main road from Boston to Spilsby. Stickney comes in the middle, and has a large and imposing church. The nave roof and clerestory are by Butterfield (1853) – indeed Butterfieldian and handsome; the tower is a rebuilding by Bassett Smith (1900), but good conservative work. In-side, however, there are Early English arcades, and – squeeze behind the organ – there is a rich Victorian window, by an unknown designer, of the Garden of Eden, all exuberant greenery and foliage, with a gushing stream and waterfall.

Stixwould An attractive church, largely a rebuilding of 1831, with a pretty tower, and containing medieval coffin lids from Stixwould Priory, old screen and benchends, and a charming little nineteenth-century organ. Abbey Farm, with its long row of sash windows, is eighteenth century, and stands on the site of the Priory, founded in the twelfth century for Cistercian nuns.

Stockwith, East see **East Stockwith**

Stoke Rochford The A1 divides the two parks of Easton and Stoke

Rochford, which comprise the parish. Easton is the home of the Lincolnshire Cholmeleys, baronets, and Stoke (the great house by Burn, now the headquarters of the National Union of Teachers) the ancestral demesne of the Turnors. The church, in Stoke village, has a Transitional tower, and a Norman and Transitional nave, around which most of the spacious Perpendicular building has been added. There are wide chancel chapels, that to the north forming the Stoke Rochford Chapel, that to the south the Easton. The former contains the large monument to Sir Edmund Turnor (1707), the latter the tomb of Henry Cholmeley (1641); there are many later monuments to both families, and an array of hatchments. There are also early monuments to Rochfords, including two brasses (1470 and 1503), and many delightful *objets d' art*, including the reredos designed by Mrs G. F. Watts, and the font cover by Christopher Turnor.

Stow Rising above the red roofs of this obscure little village, surrounded by endless flat fields to the west of the Cliff, stands this great fortress-like Anglo-Saxon and Norman church. Traditionally it is Sidnacester, the Saxon cathedral city of Lindsey, but in fact the origins of this prodigious church are uncertain. There is nothing else in England to compare with the tremendous tenth-century Saxon crossing – which was later strengthened by additional arches to carry the fourteenth-century central tower. Nave and transepts are early Norman, the chancel somewhat later. Here in 1868 Pearson skilfully rebuilt the vaulting. The first sight of this interior, upon entering the church, is one to bring the worshipper to his knees. Most of the population lives at Sturton and Pearson built the church there, brick, apsidal and bellcoted, in 1879.

Stragglethorpe In a farmyard – an enchanting little medieval church, Norman and later, with an undisturbed eighteenth-century interior, of bleached box pews, two-decker pulpit, plastered ceiling, and a splendid monument by Thomas Green of Camberwell (1697) to Sir Richard Earle, 3rd and last baronet, with a touching rhyming inscription. The Elizabethan Hall decayed quietly for two centuries, to be restored sympathetically in this.

Stroxton (*pronounced 'Strawson'*) Meadows and a pond, and a church with a saddleback tower beyond the farmyard in the fields. This was largely rebuilt by Charles Kirk in 1874, but there is Norman and Early English work within; the saddleback tower is his, and gives the whole composition a decidedly French look – delightful. Monument to William Blyth (1648).

OPPOSITE *Stow: the crossing and chancel*

Strubby Empty Marshland country: the church was practically rebuilt by Maughan and Fowler (1867), the chancel by Ewan Christian (1874); but within survives the Decorated south aisle, together with a fourteenth-century effigy, and three monuments to the Ballett family (1531, 1648, and 1703), who lived at Woodthorpe Hall, the seventeenth/eighteenth-century brick house, visible across the fields from the main road (B1373).

Stubton The medieval church was pulled down, because it was 'too near the Hall'; the neat little Gothick church of 1800 was built by Sir Robert Heron, for whom Sir Jeffry Wyatville rebuilt the Hall in 1815. The chancel was added in 1869, and the whole interior, alas, Victorianised.

Sturton, Great see **Great Sturton**

Sudbrooke A little neo-Norman church by Dobson of Newcastle (1862) – a building of considerable charm, with its vaulted chancel, and vaulted apse, its Victorian furnishings, and its Victorian glass. All this was done for the Ellisons, Lincoln bankers, whose house was demolished between the wars. Their park is now a 'garden suburb', with houses sprinkled amid the plantations. Only the Palladian gatepiers on the main road proclaim the site of a once great house.

Surfleet Prettily set on the banks of the River Glen: the leaning spire of the church (it is 6 feet out of the Perpendicular) is an awe-inspiring sight. This, and much of the church, is Decorated – but there are Perpendicular features too. The interior is attractive, with its enormous buttresses, rood screen and monuments – one to Henry Heron of Cressy Hall, MP for Boston (1730): there was a famous heronry at Cressy Hall, referred to by Gilbert White in his *Natural History.*

Sutterby A tiny medieval church, of greenstone and brick, which seems to be growing out of the earthy hillside – in the beautiful Wold country, near Langton. Long disused, it is now in the care of the Friends of Friendless Churches.

Sutterton Close to the roundabout where the A16 and A17 cross: a grand cruciform church with central tower and spire. Externally the church appears mostly Perpendicular, but the west window is Decorated, with unusual tracery. The crocketed spire was tactfully rebuilt in 1787, and the whole building somewhat over-restored by Browning in 1863. Inside, the nave is Transitional, transepts and chancel Early English, but Browning's restoration gives the whole building a certain

Sutterton (John Piper, Tate Archive)

Victorian stiffness, and the sanctuary is aglow with bright Victorian tiles. The Beridge Arms keeps alive the memory of the family of squarsons at Algarkirk, which is visible across the Fen landscape to the east.

Sutton, Long see **Long Sutton**

Sutton Bridge A long wide street leading to the Swing Bridge across the Nene: ill luck has dogged what might have been an important little port, here at the mouth of the river. The great days were in the middle of the nineteenth century, when Robert Stephenson built the first bridge, and the prosperous-looking church was built (1843). It is of flint and stone, with short chancel and sturdy west tower, all early Victorian Perpendicular.

Sutton-on-Sea Along the coast from Mablethorpe: caravans and chalets are unending. The brick church with its saddleback tower was built in 1818, to replace the original – washed away by the sea.

Sutton St Edmund A long Fen village, with a late eighteenth-century brick church with cupola-crowned west tower. Inside, box pews, varnished and numbered, west gallery, and an organ with a Gothick case. The Victorians, alas, had to meddle with the south windows.

Sutton St James The church lost its nave during the Commonwealth – tower and chancel survive, curiously separated. The chancel is Perpendicular, but the apse was added in 1879 by Bassett Smith.

Swaby A pretty Wold valley, and a little brick church of 1828, with small apse and Gothic windows. At the end of the street there is a delightful walk along the valley watered by the diminutive Great Eau.

Swallow Delightful Wold country: a stream nearby disappears into the ground – a 'swallow'. The church was over-restored in 1868; the tower is in origin Norman, but crowned with a Victorian pyramid roof; Norman nave arcade.

Swarby A small estate village on the edge of the Stone Belt: a diminutive green, and a dominating church tower, with a fine show of pinnacles and low pyramidal stone roof; on the west face of the tower is inscribed 'John Thurlow of this town. God have mercy'. This, and most of the church, are Perpendicular, somewhat Victorianised. Inside, a small, mutilated, thirteenth-century seated figure of Our Lord.

Swaton One of the lesser-known marvels of Lincolnshire – a grand cruciform church with central tower, but a stone's throw from the Bridge End Road, on the very edge of the Fens.

It is always a thrill to push open the north door, and to stand confronted by the amazing, lofty, spacious nave, its aisles almost as lofty as the nave itself, by the enormous traceried windows, and the font adorned with diapering and ball flower ornament. All this is Decorated. To turn east and look through the lower, narrower crossing arches is to see earlier work – the base of the tower, and the Early English chancel with its lancet windows, and very early traceried east window. It is a pleasure just to walk round this wonderful church, and absorb old pew ends, old stone floors, with the daylight pouring in through clear-glass windows.

In the back lanes to the west is the forgotten hamlet of Spanby. The little red brick church of 1882 has been abandoned, but there is a charming small early eighteenth-century stone manor house.

Swayfield The little church with its Early English tower, otherwise rebuilt in 1876 by F. H. Goddard, sits surrounded by farm buildings on sloping ground a few hundred yards from the main railway line: an endearing sight. Stone village.

Swinderby Woods, the Foss Way, the RAF station. The church has a notable Norman north arcade, and an extraordinary Victorian apsidal sanctuary, where the lantern in the apex sheds light on to the altar. The tower is thirteenth century, and eighteenth-century iron screens divide chancel from north chapel; there are a number of eighteenth-century monuments – one to a Disney.

Swineshead Here in the middle of the Fens King John spent several nights at Swineshead Abbey in October 1216 after losing his baggage in the Wash: nothing remains of this Cistercian house. The village is large and straggling, presided over by a magnificent Decorated and Perpendicular church; the grand Perpendicular tower is crowned with a beautiful battlemented octagon, from which rises the spire, 160 feet high. Inside, it is wide and lofty, with Decorated arcades, old roofs and floors, and a good deal of Victorian glass. The chancel was rebuilt by Stephen Lewin in 1848. (See illustration overleaf.)

Swinhope A particularly beautiful valley of the Wolds. The Hall, seat of the Alingtons, stands above its lake, a house of 1785 in white brick, with sash windows and central pediment; the pink-washed Old Rectory stands below, with its Trafalgar verandahs. Nearby is the tiny ancient church (chiefly thirteenth century) with its squat tower, and an interior filled with Alington monuments.

Swinstead Overlooking Grimsthorpe Park stands a little pavilion tower, unmistakably the work of Vanbrugh – built to enjoy the view. Swinstead is an attractive estate village of stone cottages; the Hall is the Grimsthorpe dower house. The church has a low thirteenth-century tower, a late Norman nave arcade, and a Decorated chancel and south aisle. There is a monument by Westmacott to the 5th and last Duke of Ancaster.

Syston The great house on the hill, built by Sir John Thorold, 9th baronet c. 1770, was pulled down sixty years ago; the library, built by the 10th baronet, contained one of the finest collections in England, and a copy of the very rare Mazarin Bible, when sold in 1884, fetched the largest sum for a single volume then recorded: £3,200; it went to America. When sold again a few years ago, it fetched a million. The Old Hall, with its Jacobean porch and enormous courtyard, is now the seat of the baronet. The church overlooks it, with its Norman tower (with Perpendicular pinnacled top), its Norman nave and chancel arch. There are many monuments to the family (see also Marston), and glass by Ward and Hughes, and Kempe, and delightful Comper furnishings.

Tallington The trains roar by along the Great Northern main line, on what is now one of the railway's favourite speed-trial tracks. The church is down a lane off the stone-built village street, with a Decorated west tower, and an exterior in no way exceptional. But inside it is a building full of puzzles: it is unattractively scraped, but at any rate the scraping – from the archaeological point of view – reveals the complexity of the building; for beside Early English or Decorated arcades and Perpendicular windows, there are baffling Norman (or Saxon) fragments, curiosities like the position of the tower and the extraordinary patchwork of the masonry in the transepts. The visitor can but do his own guesswork.

Tathwell A pretty village, with a small lake – whose springs are the source of the River Lud. The church stands above the lake; the tower is medieval, with an eighteenth-century brick top, and the church itself is eighteenth-century brick – its windows made Gothic in the nineteenth century. Inside there is the monument to Edward Hanby, Lord Mayor of London (1626), with kneeling figures, and a number of later Chaplin monuments.

Tattershall The vast red-brick Tudor castle keep is an astonishing and wonderful landscape feature, here in the middle of the Fens. It was built c. 1445 by Ralph Lord Cromwell, replacing a medieval castle, built in the thirteenth century. The warm red and brown brick of the castle contrasts happily with the silvery ashlar of the church, which was also founded by Lord Cromwell, in 1438, but completed after his death by William of Waynflete (his executor), Bishop of Winchester and founder of Magdalen College, Oxford – whose arms appear on the north porch. This grand, cruciform collegiate church now stands alone, denuded of

OPPOSITE *Swineshead (John Piper)*

the buildings of the college which once supported it. The light pours through the enormous clear-glass windows on this splendid somewhat threadbare interior. Wooden roofs and nave pulpit and old floors remain: a stone screen divides nave from chancel, and the north transept contains an array of brasses. The east window is half full of yellow, gold and blue glass fragments – all that remains after the rest was removed to Stamford in the eighteenth century. Even in its denuded state, a very moving building.

Tealby Even before the Second World War this pretty village began to be discovered, and new houses appeared: many are the 'desirable residences' that have appeared since. Yet it remains a beautiful spot on the slopes of the Wolds. The church stands above everything, with its grand Norman tower; the top of this is Perpendicular, as is the nave clerestory, and the south porch with its unusual window above the doorway. Inside, the nave arcades are Early English and Decorated, and the chancel is a re-modelling by James Fowler (1872). The niches are filled with monuments and inscriptions to the Tennyson-d'Eyncourts of Bayons Manor. The builder of this enormous and romantic pile (monstrously dynamited in 1965) was Charles Tennyson d'Eyncourt, Tennyson's uncle; the full story of this amazing building is told in Sir Charles Tennyson's *Alfred Tennyson* (see also Somersby).

Temple Bruer In the middle of the Heath stands an impressive Early English tower, 50 feet high, in the middle of a farmyard, all that remains of a preceptory of the Knights Templar, founded here in the reign of Henry II. Not far away is the little church of 1874, by James Fowler, solitary by the roadside.

Tetford A large village of many lanes in the beautiful Tennyson valley: the church is of the local greenstone, Decorated and Perpendicular, and contains monuments to the Dymokes. The Dymokes of Tetford were descended from the younger son of Charles II's Champion, and lived at the beautiful seventeenth and eighteenth-century house called the Mansion House; they subsequently succeeded to Scrivelsby and the Championship.

Tetney A grand Perpendicular tower, and a wide, spacious Marshland interior with Perpendicular arcades – one pier on the north side bearing a date and inscription concerning the building (1363). The chancel is a rebuilding by Withers (1861). Grimsby suburbia grows nearer.

Theddlethorpe All Saints 'The Cathedral of the Marsh' – the grandest

Theddlethorpe All Saints

Theddlethorpe All Saints: fanciful heads on parclose screen

and largest of them all, of special interest for its architecture and its furnishings. West tower with flèche, wide clerestoried nave, spacious aisles and chancel, all largely Perpendicular. The texture is wonderful, too, with brown stone, and greenstone and grey stone outside, with a glorious patching of red brick; and, inside, with ample re-use of dark Norman zigzag stone (from the earlier church) in the nave clerestory. Great wealth of old woodwork: the rood screen is gay with bright medieval colouring and eighteenth-century marbling; the parclose screens enclosing the chapels are sixteenth century, and contain remarkable heads in the spandrels, including some astonishing evil-looking faces, and others looking like the Man in the Moon wearing a nightcap, with long tassels hanging down in front. Besides all this there are splendid eighteenth-century monuments to Newcomens and Berties, a fifteenth-century brass, and (comparable with those at St Helen and Saltfleetby) an ornate and rare medieval stone reredos. This exceptional church is now in the care of the Redundant Churches Fund.

Theddlethorpe St Helen A leafy corner, and a spacious clerestoried Perpendicular church. There was much rebuilding by S. S. Teulon in 1864, but he treated the building with sympathy. Inside, its special treasure is a fourteenth-century stone reredos, comparable with those at Theddlethorpe All Saints and Saltfleetby, but more elaborate, and remarkably preserved.

Thimbleby A pretty village street of thatched, whitewashed cottages leads up to the church – almost entirely rebuilt by James Fowler in 1879; it is of greenstone, with a small octagonal tower and spirelet; a few medieval fragments within.

Thoresby, North see **North Thoresby**

Thoresby, South see **South Thoresby**

Thoresway In a long and pretty valley of the Wolds: the church with its little bell turret was almost rebuilt by Fowler in 1879, but he incorporated one Norman arch, and the thirteenth-century nave arcades.

Thorganby A remote and beautiful spot. The church, chiefly of thirteenth-century date, was sensitively restored in 1900, and is beautifully furnished: old benchends; Comper windows.

Thornton A handful of houses, and a little Victorianised church of greenstone, with tiled roof and overhanging eaves, tastefully done up by Ewan Christian in 1890. The most remarkable thing is the set of eighteenth-century wrought-iron hatpegs on the walls of the nave: there is accommodation for thirty-two hats!

Thornton Curtis Thornton Abbey, founded for Augustinian canons in 1139, lies to the north – with its greatest of all monastic gatehouses, and the exquisite fragment of its chapter house. The parish church stands in the village – an Early English building, with a pinnacled Perpendicular top to its tower. Inside, the exceptionally broad nave and aisles are

Thornton Curtis: black marble Tournai font

impressive; so are the Early English arcades, so is the south door with its medieval ironwork, so is the Jacobean pulpit. But most of all it is the black Tournai marble front which makes the church of exceptional interest. It is one of only seven in England, and comparable with those at Lincoln and Winchester. Thornton Hall is a handsome brick house, built by Sir Rowland Winn (of Nostell) in the early eighteenth century, with lower, later, side pavilions.

Thornton-le-Moor A remote spot, and a forlorn little church; but it possesses several features of great antiquity – a Norman bellcote and south doorway, a fragment of an Anglo-Saxon cross shaft, and an unusual Decorated clerestory of tiny quatrefoil windows.

Thorpe on the Hill Not much of a hill. The little church has a low capped tower, almost entirely rebuilt by C. G. Hare, Bodley's partner, in 1912. The tower is of 1722, but contains a small blocked Norman window.

Thorpe St Peter On the edge of Marsh and Fen; the church stands in trees, with a low pinnacled Decorated tower, and a clerestoried nave of this date. There is a striking Early English font, and a Jacobean pulpit.

Threckingham A strong, sturdy Decorated broach spire, and a long dignified nave with Norman and Decorated arcades: it is a big, spacious interior, and at the west end are three enormous tombs, popularly supposed to be the tombs of the three Danish kings killed near here at the Battle of Stow Green in 870 – from whom, it is held, the village takes its name. In reality they are of fourteenth-century date. But the gaily painted inn sign – The Three Kings – carries on the old story.

Thurlby *(near Bourne)* A large village on the edge of the Fen, and a

Thurlby (near Bourne) and (right) Threckingham. (Both John Piper, Tate Archive.)

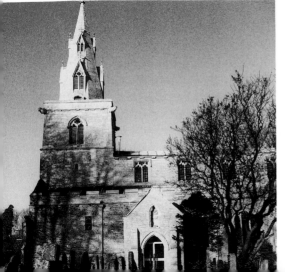
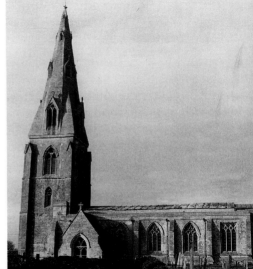

Thurlby (near Bourne): the interior

blunt little spire on a cruciform church of chapels and vistas. The base of
the tower is pre-Norman; so may be some of the rest of the building,
but there is much later work of various dates, and Victorian furnishing.
Very colourful Victorian glass, some by O'Connor.

Thurlby *(by Lincoln)* A tiny village lost in the woods to the south of the
Foss Way: a small, ancient church (twelfth to fourteenth century) with a
modest tower, and an interior dark and mysterious, full of woodwork,
and monuments to the Bromheads, baronets, a distinguished military
family who have lived at the Hall since the end of the seventeenth
century.

Timberland A village of tortuous corners: there is a brick Wesleyan Chapel of 1878, spruce and well maintained, a charming Victorian (former) school bearing the arms of the Whichcotes, and a public house called The Pennyfarthing. The church has a bold Early English tower, with a Transitional arch into the nave – with a later Early English arch inserted, no doubt to strengthen it when the present tower was built – and Early English nave arcades. The eighteenth-century plaster ceiling is attractive: it is a pity that it has been painted bright blue.

Thorpe Tilney Hall is a delightful mid-eighteenth-century house of mellow red brick, with cupola-crowned stables, and an enormous walled garden complete with contemporary summer house – built by the Whichcotes. It is now the home of F. M. Stockdale, founder of the Pavilion Opera Company, and Francis Johnson has built for him an exquisite opera house, its windows filled with John Piper glass. Here in the season, and elsewhere at other times, his Company delights us with its performances.

Toft-next-Newton Next door to Newton-by-Toft (of course): a little bell-coted church by Hodgson Fowler (1891), containing fragmentary remains of the early church, and part of an Anglo-Saxon cross in the churchyard.

Torksey The old pronunciation is 'Torsey'. A main-road village, at the junction of the Foss Dyke and the River Trent. Much of the church is of 1821, but the tower is Perpendicular, and inside there is an Early English arcade with beautiful stiff leaf capitals. On the river bank stands the romantic ruin of Torksey Castle, an Elizabethan mansion of stone and brick, built by Sir Robert Jermyn, with gaping windows and four octagonal turrets, all burnt in the Civil War; but its façade still stands like a stage set, ready for some tragic play to be enacted here. In the early nineteenth century William Billingsley established his porcelain factory nearby, and made the rare 'Torksey Ware', now so greatly valued by collectors.

Torrington, East see **East Torrington**

Torrington, West see **West Torrington**

Tothill The little church of 1778, of brick on a medieval stone base, has been wickedly destroyed in recent years. It stood on the Toot Hill (motte and bailey), a historic site, from which the place took its name.

Toynton, High see **High Toynton**

Toynton, Low see **Low Toynton**

Toynton All Saints Perched on the last shelf of the Wolds, looking down a winding lane to the Fens, stands what appears to be a brick eighteenth-century church with a low tower. In fact, inside, it displays its true medieval self, for embedded in its nave walls are the Transitional and Early English arcades. Excellent restoration of 1904 has created the attractive interior which we now see, with good choir stalls, rood screen and barrel roof.

Toynton St Peter Below the southern edge of the Wolds. The church has a greenstone Perpendicular tower, but was otherwise over-restored by James Fowler in 1876. Fourteenth-century north arcade.

Trusthorpe Bungalows and caravans are continuous along the coast from Mablethorpe. The church is not far from the sea, and has a seventeenth-century brick tower, an early nineteenth-century nave, and an early twentieth-century chancel. The medieval chancel arch has survived all changes.

Tydd St Mary On the very frontier: Cambridgeshire to the south, Norfolk to the east. The church has a Perpendicular brick tower with stone spire, and a brick nave clerestory: all else is of stone. Inside, the nave has Transitional arcades; there is an alabaster effigy of William de Tidde (1395), and of two eighteenth-century monuments to the Trafford family one is by Rysbrack (1741).

Uffington The churchyard gates were erected in 1679 by the Hon. Charles Bertie, second son of the 2nd Earl of Lindsey, who bought Uffington in 1673: opposite stands the even more magnifical garden gate to the house, with grand gatepiers crowned with urns; together they form quite a theatrical approach to the church. This is an impressive, spacious building, outwardly all Perpendicular, with lofty crocketed spire with low flying buttressses. Inside, the nave is Early English, but there is much rich Victorian adornment (by E. Browning, 1865), and Victorian glass by Wailes and Clayton and Bell. Two early seventeenth-century monuments in the chancel; late seventeenth-century candelabrum. Uffington House, like a smaller version of Belton, was tragically burnt in 1904; but Casewick (in its park to the north-east), seat of the Trollopes – now flats – survives, part Jacobean, part eighteenth-century Gothick; an enchanting house.

Ulceby *(near Alford)* A pretty Wold village, and a rather odd little brick church of 1826, in a beautiful position.

Ulceby *(near Grimsby)* The church boasts an Early English tower and Perpendicular spire – and spires in North Lincolnshire are not common. A good spacious church, Early English and Decorated, somewhat Victorianised.

Upton-cum-Kexby In the flat countryside between Gainsborough and the Cliff; the church has an eighteenth-century tower: the rest is in origin medieval (late Norman tympanum to south door, thirteenth-century north arcade), but much rebuilt by Ewan Christian in 1867, and James Fowler a decade later.

Usselby A tiny secret secluded backwater, off the main road from Market Rasen to Caistor; there is no signpost to the place – only a hanging painted notice proclaiming USSELBY at the corner. There is a handful of houses and farm buildings, and a little late Georgian stone church with wooden cupola.

Utterby A backwater off the A16 (Louth to Grimsby) – with a number of attractive old houses. The church has escaped the heavy hand of the Victorian restorer, and its many-textured exterior – of chalk, ironstone and brick – is charming. It is the same inside, all Decorated or Perpendicular, with a fourteenth-century effigy, a number of eighteenth-and nineteenth-century monuments, some fragments of ancient glass, and a pretty thirteenth-century canopied niche in the north aisle.

Waddingham A village attractively set around a green – the church on rising ground to the east. A Perpendicular tower, and an over-restored exterior (1862); inside, Early English arcades in the nave, the chancel mostly Victorian. Wide views towards the Ancholme, and the Wolds beyond.

Waddington Dominated by the RAF station, a stone village now ruined by commonplace housing. The medieval church was obliterated by a landmine during the war, and replaced by a new building (by Skipper and Partners of Lowestoft) in 1954: a somewhat cold and cheerless barn.

Waddingworth A tiny church in a farmyard, behind the big farmhouse which stands in the middle of no man's land among enormous fields between Bardney and Horncastle. A little building, medieval and Georgian, with triple chancel arch and furnishings by H. F. Traylen (1913). Now disused. The bell fell on the last Sunday before war broke out in 1914, and again in 1939. When next, they wonder?

OPPOSITE *Ulceby (near Grimsby)*

Wainfleet It is difficult now to conceive of Wainfleet as an important port – but such it was, and more ancient than Boston. It is an odd little town, now two miles from the sea, to be venerated as the birthplace of William of Waynflete (c. 1395), Bishop of Winchester, Chancellor of England, first Provost of Eton, founder of Magdalen College, Oxford. Magdalen College School, here, which he also founded, is the only distinguished building in the town, an imposing Tudor brick structure – related to his buildings at Eton. The church is disappointing: after the collapse of the grand medieval church, this rather plain building of white brick was erected, with meagre Perpendicular features (1821). Wainfleet is now famous chiefly for its brewery – a charming building with early nineteenth-century balconied house to the street, a windmill behind, where 'Bateman's Good Honest Ales' are brewed, still by the Bateman family.

Wainfleet St Mary Through the rookery and past the beech and yew hedges, remote and hard to find in meandering dyked lanes stands the church – 1½ miles from the village of its name; but it is worth the

Wainfleet St Mary

Wainfleet St Mary: the tower

search. There is Norman work in the base of the tower – the rest is Early English and Perpendicular; the nave is Early English, but much of the rest of the building is Perpendicular. The interior is devout and beautiful, with rood screen and other recent furnishings; there are eighteenth-century altar rails, and a monument to Edward Barkham, who bequeathed all his property here to Bethlehem Hospital (1732).

Walcot Astonishing, lofty, crocketed broach spire, a powerful landmark. Like the spire, the church is externally Decorated; there is an ornate little priest's doorway to the south-east chapel, and a seventeenth-century panelled door in the south porch. Inside there are Early English arcades, an Early English font, old benchends, and, through the clear glass of the east window, a view of the splendid weeping beech outside. Altogether a church of great charm.

Walcott, see Billinghay

Walesby A pretty spot at the foot of the Wolds. In the village itself a church of 1914 by Temple Moore, a building of considerable interest, as he has divided the nave with a lofty central arcade – inspired, no doubt by Caythorpe (*q.v.*). High up on the Wold stands the old church, abandoned when the new church was built, but rescued in the 1930s by that champion of old churches – before the Lincolnshire Old Churches Trust was founded – Canon N. S. Harding. It is a building of the greatest charm, with squat Early English tower, Transitional nave arcades, Early English chancel. Moreover it is beautifully furnished: pews and rood screen are painted white, and the Jacobean pulpit came from Kirkstead.

Waltham A large towny village on the outskirts of Grimsby – a windmill in full working order, an over-restored church (in origin early fourteenth century), with a Perpendicular font, and a charming brass of Joanna Waltham (1420), with demi-figures of her, her son and her daughter, in the south window of the chancel.

Washingborough Along the River Witham, east of Lincoln – the view de Wint loved to paint. Washingborough is now a large dormitory village, bursting with well-to-do houses. An imposing church, with Perpendicular-crowned Early English tower and nave, and Decorated chancel – all restored by Scott in 1860. There are a number of interesting monuments, especially those to Sir Peter Eure (1612), and his son Ralph (1664), seventeenth-century altar rails, an exotic chandelier, and an unusual rood beam with figures.

OPPOSITE *Crocket perches on the broach spire at Walcot*

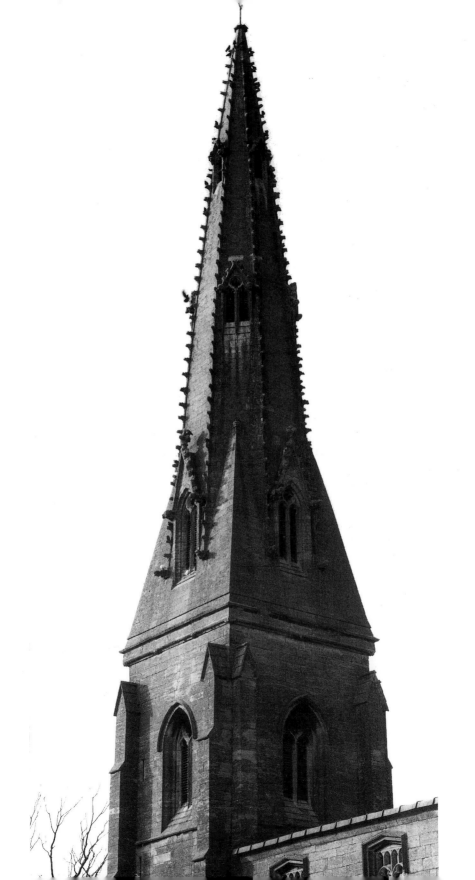

Waythe The traveller along the A16 (Louth to Grimsby) sees a venerable Anglo-Saxon tower, a short distance off to the east: what will surprise him is the James Fowler church (1861) which envelops it on all sides – for it is a central tower, and narrow arches lead through from the nave and into the chancel. This is amazing – apsidal, with tile decoration and monuments to the Haigh family (of Grainsby), all shining and polychromatic like a Turkish bath.

Welbourn Its extraordinary humped spire – its entasis even more pronounced than that at Caythorpe – dominates the level countryside under the Cliff; nave aisles and porch are all distinguished Decorated work, the chancel an uninspired rebuilding of 1854. Of special interest is the tablet to Field Marshal Sir William Robertson, who was gardener's boy at the rectory, and rose from being a private to becoming CIGS in 1915.

Welby A stone village in pretty countryside, and a distinguished and interesting church, with a diminutive Early English tower and broach spire, Perpendicular clerestoried nave with pinnacled parapet, and Perpendicular south porch. Some old woodwork inside.

Well The most beautiful setting for any house or church in Lincolnshire: James Bateman, brother of the 1st Lord Bateman (of Shobdon), built the house in 1725, and landscaped the park with its wells and lakes. As an eye-catcher he built the little Palladian church on the hill, aligned on the front door: it is perfect outside – and in, with its original furnishing and plasterwork. In the portico it is possible to sit and survey the view – of the house with its restrained pedimented façade, the garden and the park, the lakes, and, in the distance, the sea.

Wellingore The church looks splendid, perched on the edge of the Cliff – especially so when floodlit at night. It is all Decorated and Perpendicular, with its blunt spire and lofty clerestoried nave. Inside, old benchends, fifteenth-century tomb of Sir Richard de Buslingthorpe. Next door, the Hall is a late eighteenth-century house built by the Neviles of Aubourn (*q.v.*), now flats. The Roman Catholic chapel, by J. MacVicar Anderson (1876), is lavish Victorian Norman, with glass by Burlison and Grylls.

Welton by Lincoln New bungalows everywhere: a dormitory village. The church has an eighteenth-century tower – the rest looks all nineteenth-century outside (rebuilt by E. J. Willson, 1824), but retains its medieval arcades within.

St Margaret's, Well

Welton-le-Marsh An eighteenth-century brick church on a medieval stone base, the windows Gothicised in the restoration of 1891 – the Victorians could not leave things alone; eighteenth-century tower. The church sits prettily in its churchyard above the Marshland village.

Welton-le-Wold A fourteenth-century tower, and a well-proportioned, finely detailed church of 1850, overlooking a lush valley close to Louth.

West Ashby A greenstone church with a Perpendicular tower – but like so many churches in these parts over-restored in the last century (1873). Norman south doorway, Early English nave. Next door stands a particularly attractive Queen Anne brick house, with a front door from Captain Cook's house in London.

West Barkwith The church was shamefully destroyed a few years ago: with its Perpendicular tower (carefully rebuilt as recently as 1930), and modest nave and chancel (restored by R. J. Withers in 1867), it was a lovable landmark, a Christian symbol, on the road from Wragby to Louth. A disgrace.

West Butterwick A large Dutchlike village on the west bank of the Trent, looking across to East Butterwick opposite. The church is of 1841, by Charles Briggs, Gothic, in white brick, with a small octagonal spire, and period interior.

West Deeping The elegant Perpendicular spire is a familiar and much-loved landmark from the railway – the first Lincolnshire church after crossing the frontier from Peterborough; here the River Welland divides the counties. West Deeping is a stone village; the church stands close to the mill, down a narrow lane off the main street. The exterior is largely Perpendicular and handsome, but inside there is an Early English nave and Decorated chancel. Butterfield rstored the church in 1876, and there is interesting decoration by him in the chancel.

West Halton Stone walls, old sycamores, meadows. The little church sits delightfully in its simple setting, with a modest Perpendicular tower, the rest largely rebuilt in 1692 after a fire, tactfully restored in 1876. A very small village near the Humber.

West Halton

West Keal The church with its tall pinnacled Perpendicular tower looks magnificent, perched on the southernmost shelf of the Wolds. The *Shell* film about the Fens, made a few years ago, started here in the porch, with its breathtaking view of the enormous sweep of the Fens, Boston Stump in the distance below – and concluded with the organ playing under the octagon at Ely Cathedral. The tower fell in 1881, but was carefully rebuilt; the south porch is distinguished work of the Decorated period, but the glory of the building is the nave with its Decorated arcades, and fascinating, unusual capitals, displaying dragons fighting, a fox stealing a goose, and countrywomen bursting out of their bodices. The chancel was rebuilt by Street in 1867. The village is below.

West Rasen Two miles west of Middle Rasen, has a fourteenth-century packhorse bridge, and a large and handsome church. The prominent tower is early fourteenth century, with unusual embattled pinnacles; the Norman north arcade is blocked up, and the south arcade is Early English. It is a spacious interior. The building was sympathetically restored by E. J. Willson in 1829.

West Torrington 'Church 1100, restored 1860' proclaims the optimistic notice hanging at the gate. It is a modest little church with a double bellcote. There is little to see of 1100; it was all restored and much rebuilt by R. J. Withers in 1860, but is attractive in its quiet way. Norman font; churchyard cross.

Westborough A wonderful dead-end village; the lane, dotted with old red cottages and larger houses set back in generous gardens, leads nowhere but the River Witham, the church close to its bank. A stately building, thirteenth and fourteenth century, with clear-glass windows, a stone altar in the sacristy, old screen, pulpit and benchends, eighteenth-century monuments to the Hall family, rectors of the parish, Time and Death on the west wall, and a plain eighteenth-century tower, it stands gracious and a little forlorn in its churchyard of old headstones and chestnut trees. The Old Rectory is very handsome with its long sash windows, a late seventeenth- and early eighteenth-century house of warm red brick.

Weston St Mary As pure architecture this is one of the most precious of Lincolnshire churches, a perfect Early English building with some later, Decorated, details, and a Perpendicular west tower. The pleasures begin with the south porch, and continue with the five-bay nave, with its piers with detached shafts and stiff-leaf capitals, and the chancel with its delicate lancets. Pearson restored the church in 1886. Fen countryside: a signpost pointing to a specially flat stretch of country is inexplicably labelled 'To Weston Hills'.

Whaplode A wonderful church. There is a long nave of seven bays with grand Norman and Transitional arcades, an Early English and Decorated tower (with little eighteenth-century pinnacles), and everywhere clear glass – though the yellow 'cathedral' glass of the east window is somewhat depressing. The early seventeenth-century ten-poster tomb of Sir Anthony Irby, with his and his wife's recumbent effigies, resembles the Wray tomb at Ashby-cum-Fenby (*q.v.*); there is a seventeenth-century pulpit, and eighteenth-century reredos. A fragment of Irby Hall survives, now a farmhouse. Flat Fen countryside.

Whaplode: tomb of Sir Anthony Irby

Wilksby: 'small and remote'

Whitton The straight, solitary road from West Halton leads to Whitton, and no further: the village is perched dramatically above the Humber. The church has a Norman tower, but much of the rest is a rebuilding by Bassett Smith (1897). Delightful grassy churchyard, full of old headstones – a relief after the pagan 'gardens', denuded of their graves, which surround several nearby churches.

Wickenby G. G. Scott, junior built the tower in 1868, and there has been some Victorian restoration – but this is a delightful medieval church, Early English and Decorated and Perpendicular, exceptionally well furnished, and a pleasure to visit. The rood screen is Perpendicular, there is a beautiful reredos of 1929, a little old glass, and an interesting brass of 1635.

Wigtoft A Fenland church of considerable architectural merit, outwardly all Decorated and Perpendicular, with Perpendicular tower and short spirelet, and handsome clerestoried Perpendicular nave; inside a few Norman fragments are incorporated in the Early English base of the tower, and the nave arcades are Decorated. Enormous Fen fields all round.

Wildsworth The little church of white brick, built in 1836 by Charles Briggs, overlooking the Trent, has been demolished.

Wilksby Small and remote: a tiny church of brick and greenstone, in origin medieval, but mostly eighteenth century, with Gothic windows with wooden tracery. Delightful headstones in the churchyard.

Willingham, North see **North Willingham**

Willingham, South see **South Willingham**

Willingham-by-Stow Remote countryside; outside the church looks all Victorian, and is indeed the work of Brodrick and Smith (1880). But there are Norman fragments inside, and the tower itself is Decorated.

Willoughby A leafy, pretty village, where the Wolds slope down to the Marsh. The great Willoughby de Eresby family take their name from here, migrating over the centuries to Eresby (see Spilsby), and then to Grimsthorpe (see Edenham), where, happily, they still live. A grand Perpendicular church of Marshland character, wide yet lofty. A recent monument, and still more recent stained-glass windows, commemorate Captain John Smith, a native of Willoughby and founder of Virginia; his portrait adorns the sign of the Willoughby Arms, together with the escutcheon of the Willoughbys.

Willoughby, Scot see **Scot Willoughby**

Willoughby, Silk see **Silk Willoughby**

Willoughton Below the Cliff. The church is mostly of 1794, with a squat tower crowned with a low pyramid roof with ball-shaped finial. The nave is wide, with a flat plaster ceiling: only the chancel arch and a little masonry in the chancel survive from the medieval building. Jacobean tomb of Nicholas Sutton (1602).

Wilsford A stone village in a valley – by-passed by the main Grantham-Sleaford road, with an interesting church with a slender Perpendicular spire. There is Saxon, Norman and Early English work within; the chancel is Decorated, and there is a superb traceried Decorated east window.

Wilsthorpe Its comic little pinnacled exterior may deceive the unwary, and give the impression of a Victorian monstrosity. In fact this is a charming little church of 1715 – but in 1863 James Fowler did his best to ruin it, trying to Gothicise it, putting on the absurd little shingled spire, and 'lombardising' all the windows. Poor Wilsthorpe.

Winteringham A large village, or decayed little town, on the hillside surveying the Humber bank. There are wide views across the river to Yorkshire. The church lies at the far end: the tower appears Perpendicular, but contains Norman masonry, and the nave is composed of distinguished Norman (or Transitional) arcades; Early English chancel with long narrow lancets.

Winteringham: close to the Humber bank. RIGHT *Winterton.*

Winterton A large village close to the Humber. A Victorian lamp, guarding the entrance to the churchyard, is cheerfully dated AD 1203. The church is a splendid building, with an Anglo-Saxon tower (with Perpendicular pinnacled top), and thirteenth-century nave with interesting and unusual arcades. There are transepts and wide aisles dating from the early fourteenth century. Beautifully furnished interior with excellent Victorian glass by Kempe and others.

Winthorpe An imposing Perpendicular Marshland church, a mere two miles from Skegness, but somehow remote. Ornate south porch, battlemented clerestory, west tower, and bellcote for the sanctus at the east end of the nave; the interior is specially rich in woodwork: rood screen, parclose screens, benchends, chancel stalls, the roof adorned with bosses. A rewarding church.

Wispington Its pretty little Victorian spire is a charming landmark across the enormous fields, here in no man's land; by J. B. Atkinson, but used now as the Diocesan Furniture Store, for furnishings from redundant churches. Sad. But at any rate it can be restored, when the Age of Faith returns.

Witham, North see **North Witham**

Witham, South see **South Witham**

Witham-on-the-Hill: Perpendicular nave, Georgian tower and spire

Witham-on-the-Hill An attractive stone village, with a large and impressive church. The great thing is the eighteenth-century tower, with its urns and short spire, forming the south transept. It is dated 1738, and is the work of George Portwood of Stamford. The nave is late Norman, with a Perpendicular clerestory, the chancel Perpendicular; there is a modern rood screen, and the painted panels, now restored to the church, are portions of the ancient screen, recovered from an antique shop in Lincoln. The Hall, in origin eighteenth century but enlarged in the early twentieth, was long the home of the Johnson family, descendants of Archdeacon Johnson, founder of Oakham and Uppingham Schools. It is now a prep school.

Withcall A beautiful spot in the Wolds: the old railway line from Horncastle to Louth ran through this valley. Compact little bellcoted stone church by Sir A. Blomfield (1882).

Withern Smart bijou residences line the lane to the church – but this is all forlorn and abandoned. The nave retains its Perpendicular arcades, but otherwise is early nineteenth-century Gothick, and the windows are – or were– filled with bright enamelled glass; the chancel is mediev-al. The whole building is now derelict, the font transferred to the graveyard, and used as a bird bath. Disgraceful. (See Introduction.)

Wold Newton A pretty valley and a tiny village of brick and stone. James Fowler's little church (1860), with its apse and bellcote, sits on the hillside against the woods; inside, a painted rood beam, some panels of seventeenth-century Continental glass, and many objects of piety.

Wood Enderby Remote, obscure little village, at the back of beyond, somewhere near Claxby Pluckacre: a modest medieval church, largely Victorianised – with an unexpected broach spire (Victorian, of course). Declared redundant, the church is now in private hands. At any rate, it is good to know that it is safe.

Woodhall, Old see **Old Woodhall**

Woodhall Spa 'That most unexpected Bournemouth-like settlement in the middle of Lincolnshire', as John Betjeman described it. Here among pine trees and silver birches and rhododendrons, grand late Victorian half-timbered hotels and the celebrated golf course, will be found not only the old Spa, the Kinema in the Woods, and the Tea House in the Woods, but a church of 1893 by Hodgson Fowler in soft red brick, with brick traceried windows, and beautifully furnished interior. It has all the atmosphere of a well-to-do church in a seaside resort on the South Coast – indeed, as a friend once said to the author, driving down the Broadway, 'You almost feel that the sea front is just ahead – beyond the pine trees.'

Woolsthorpe A beautiful setting, below Belvoir Castle (just in Leices-tershire), with a long village street climbing the hill. The church is of 1847, by G. G. Place, impressive and commodious, built of the local deep golden ironstone: grand views across the valley to the ducal towers of Belvoir.

Wootton The main road from Barrow to Brigg: an attractive village with pond and village green. The church has Perpendicular tower and Early English nave – all somewhat over-restored. Wootton Hall stands in its small park, a handsome late eighteenth-century brick house, with pedimented front, Doric porch, and Venetian window.

Worlaby Under the western slopes of the Wolds: a church largely rebuilt by W. Scott Champion in 1873, but retaining an Anglo-Saxon tower arch,and fourteenth-century nave arcades. Monument to John, 1st Lord Belasyse of Worlaby, Royalist commander, whose seventeenth-century brick almshouses are nearby.

Wragby An enormous wide Market Place, the Turnor Arms, Sir Edmund Turnor's almshouses (founded 1677, rebuilt 1840), the parish church of 1838 (by W. A. Nicholson) of the Commissioners' type, in white brick – that is all, but Wragby has character, and is the gateway to the Wolds, and much wonderful, unknown country.

Wrangle Another imposing church on the road from Boston to Wainfleet – externally mostly Perpendicular; but within the porch is an Early English doorway, and the nave arcades are Decorated, as is the chancel. But the great interest of the church is the quantity of four-teenth-century glass, with rich deep colours; no other church in the county can boast so much. Brass to John Reade, merchant of the staple at Calais (1503), and elaborate tomb, with recumbent effigies, to his great-grandson Sir John Reade (1626); Jacobean pulpit.

Wrawby Dangerously near Brigg: much suburban housing. But the church is ancient, though heavily restored. The tower is thirteenth century, the nave fourteenth; the tomb of Sir Robert Tyrwhitt (1548) is of interest, though it has lost its brasses. There is a splendid post mill, with its four sails – restored in 1965 in memory of Lady Winifrede Elwes (see Elsham).

Wroot A bleak little outpost of Lincolnshire, on the westernmost edge of the Isle of Axholme, with vast bleak vistas everywhere. The little red brick church, rebuilt in 1878, stands on a hummock; John Wesley was curate to his father here, 1728-30.

Wyberton The approach from Boston is terrible, with villas and bunga-lows crowding along the main road. But round the church some charm remains, with stately trees in the Park – with its spendid eighteenth-century house, built as the rectory – and the distinguished church, externally all Perpendicular. But inside there are delicate clustered Early English columns in the nave, and a small Georgian apsidal chancel.

Wyham Up the long drive to Wyham House – and on the left stands the little church, bellcoted and somewhat over-restored; but there is her-ringbone masonry in the chancel wall, so its antiquity is certain. It is now redundant, but privately owned and cared for.

Wrangle: fourteenth-century glass – 'The Resurrection' (John Piper, Tate Archive)

Wyville A pretty hamlet in the stone uplands close to the Leicestershire border, with a charming little bellcoted white brick Gothic church, built in 1857 by the Gregorys of Harlaxton. The capacious font is attached to the west wall, like a big washbasin.

Yarburgh Lonely Marshland country. The church is of interest as having been rebuilt after a fire in 1405. So it is Perpendicular throughout, with an embattled tower, with notable carvings in the spandrels of the west doorway. The south aisle has disappeared; otherwise it is all of a piece, with a Perpendicular screen under the tower, and some old benchends. Now in the care of the Redundant Churches Fund.

Glossary

apse Semicircular or polygonal east end of church.

ashlar Masonry of finely finished even blocks.

aumbry Cupboard, usually in north wall of sanctuary, to hold the Blessed Sacrament, or sacred vessels.

Baroque Large scale, forceful and original treatment of Renaissance architecture, associated with Vanbrugh, Hawksmoor and Archer.

boss Carved stone at intersection of the ribs of a vault.

box pew Enclosed pew with door and high partitions, much favoured in eighteenth century.

broach spire Earliest type of spire, where the spire rises direct from the tower without parapet or pinnacles; the 'broach' is the sloping triangular piece of masonry connecting the angle of the square tower with the adjacent face of the octagonal spire.

capital The crown of the column.

cartouche Decorative tablet for inscription or coat of arms.

chancel The eastern limb of a church.

cinquefoil Five-leaved decoration in tracery.

clerestory Top stage of nave or chancel, lit by windows.

Coade stone Artificial stone manufactured in the late eighteenth and early nineteenth century by the Coade family in Lambeth.

collegiate church Church served by college of canons or prebendaries.

corbel A block, usually of stone, projecting from a wall to support an arch or vault.

Corinthian see *orders*.

cornice Horizontal projection at the top of a wall.

crocket Small carved ornament on the side of a spire or pinnacle.

crossing The intersection of nave, choir and transepts in a cruciform church.

crypt Vaulted chamber below church.

curvilinear Later Decorated tracery of flowing pattern.

Decorated The Decorated style (first half of fourteenth century).

dog-tooth Small pyramidal carved ornament in late Norman and Early English architecture.

Doric see *orders*.

Early English The earliest English Gothic style (thirteenth century).

Easter sepulchre Carved and usually elaborately decorated recess on the north side of sanctuary, where the Blessed Sacrament was placed on Good Friday.

fan vault see *vault.*

flèche Small timber or lead-covered spire.

flying buttress Buttress in the form of an arch or demi-arch to support the thrust of a high vault.

geometrical Earliest form of Decorated tracery, composed of geometrical patterns.

Gothick Fanciful eighteenth-century form of Gothic.

groined vault see *vault.*

hatchment Corruption of 'achievement'; painted board depicting a deceased person's coat of arms, displayed first on his house, then removed to the church.

Ionic see *orders.*

lancet Narrow pointed arched window, characteristic of Early English architecture.

lierne see *vault.*

misericord Projecting ledge on underneath of hinged seat of stall, to support the occupant standing.

nave Western limb of a church.

Norman Norman architecture, the English version of Romanesque.

ogee Design of an arch or window incorporating both convex and concave curves.

orders The Classical orders in Greek or Roman architecture. Doric – Greek Doric: solid column with simple cushion capital and no base; Roman Doric: narrower column, with base and cushion capital; Tuscan Doric: a later plain and severely designed version of Roman Doric. Ionic: elegant column, with ram's-horn capital. Corinthian: graceful column, with base and elaborately carved capital of acanthus leaves.

Palladian Architecture based on the principles of Andrea Palladio (1518-80).

pediment Classical low-pitched version of the Gothic gable.

Perpendicular The Perpendicular style, the latest phase of Gothic architecture in England, c.1350-1550.

piscina Recess with basin and drain, for washing the sacred vessels.

quatrefoil Four-leaved decoration in tracery.

quoin Dressed corner stone.

reredos Carved screen behind altar; altarpiece.

rib vault See *vault.*

Romanesque In England usually termed 'Norman'.

rood Crucifix; rood loft, rood screen – loft, screen, supporting a rood.

sanctuary Space surrounding the altar.

Saxon Pre-Conquest English architecture.

sedilia Stone or wooden seats for officiating priests in sanctuary.

spandrel Triangular space between two arches, or between an arch and adjoining pillar.

springers The base stem of a vault, springing from a pillar or wall.

stiff-leaf Carved foliage, typical of the Early English style.

tabernacle Receptacle for housing Blessed Sacrament.

three-decker Three-tiered pulpit, with reading desk, stall and pulpit above one another.

tierceron see *vault.*

transept The north and south extending limbs of a cruciform church.

Transitional Transitional Norman: the transition from Norman to Gothic.

trefoil Three-leaved decoration in tracery.

triforium Arcaded story above the arches and below the clerestory in a major church.

tympanum Space between the lintel of a doorway and the arch above, often containing elaborate carving.

vault Arched covering of space in stone (or brick, or wood); barrel vault: a vault built in one continuous arch; groined vault: the intersection of such vaults (Norman); rib vault: the simplest form of cross-vaulting (late Norman and Early English); tierceron vault: employing secondary ribs from wall to central boss (Early English); lierne vault: the use of small decorative ribs, for ornamental rather than structural purposes (Decorated); fan vault: the latest phase of Gothic vaulting, where fan-shaped panelled ribs extend in equal lengths from wall to centre of roof (Perpendicular).

Venetian window Palladian triple window, the central opening arched.

vesica window Oval window, with pointed head and foot – the derivation is from *vesica piscis* 'fish bladder', representing ICHTHUS.

Index